So, you want to be a Medium?

A journey of discovery

So, you want to be a Medium?

A journey of discovery

Edited by Vivienne Neal
Proof read by Gordon Smith
Cover by Philip K

Thanks

With great thanks to my husband Gordon, who has given me the strength and loving support to finish this project despite the setbacks since it began in 2010?

He was there to encourage me when the stuffing was knocked out and there to pick me up, dust me down again, and push me forward.

Words cannot express my gratitude to my spirit team of workers, Alchemides, Esmeralda and my connection to my own family in the spirit world.

My Grandson Harry who departed this world in August 20th 2010 leaving us with a great hole to fill, thank you for your visits to me during times of trouble.

I love you all, family truly matters, and without you I would not have fulfilled my dream xx

"To love someone deeply gives you strength. Being loved by someone deeply gives you courage"
Lao Tzu (600- 531 BCE)

So, you want to be a Medium?

A journey of discovery

Contents

“Someday perhaps the inner light will shine forth from us, and then we’ll need no other light”

Johann Wolfgang von Goethe (1749-1832)

About the Author

Angel Anne

Is an Intuitive astrology columnist and author as well as student of the universe, A Reiki Master and Light Therapy Practioner and teaches that working with spirit must come from the heart. She runs workshops on developing your spirit to satisfy your own needs to recognise we are individuals on our path of enlightenment.

Her shows are renowned for her straight talking approach giving proof of the continued existence of the human soul and connect to those in the spirit worlds with accuracy and humour.

Previously she worked in the corporate world as a product development manager. In 1998 an awakening of her gifts propelled her into a world of feeling and love, the opposite of what her life had been, her life until that point had been an illusion, that illusion was the material existence she had been living, as only love continues, our souls come with learning in mind they come with no possessions and leave with no possessions only soul growth and the love they have met and grown whilst here on earth, only love is real everything else is an illusion.

Personal Introduction.

Born in May, my sun sign is Taurus, my ascendant is Leo and my moon in Virgo means I am grounded, forthright and pragmatic and a little dramatic from time to time! I am also a nurturer and earth mother who is always fussing (at times) and trying to help people find their way. I am the oldest of six children, a natural bossy boots, my mother says, I have been bossing her around since I was two years old!

I am a mother of two grown up children and have two grandchildren.

I am a natural medium; it has been passed down from my mother as she has seen spirit all her life, and her mother before that. My father's Grandmother is from the Irish Gypsies and was very psychic so I have this gene too, as well as many others I would rather not have.

I have always connected to the spirit world, since I was a small child. I remember seeing and talking to people, who I always thought were actually real. It was only when I was around eight years old that I realised the visitors that my mum talked of visiting her (in the night) were the same ones who visited me, and they mostly came just before sleep or while I was playing quietly, alone, never when there was anyone around. When I asked my mother why this happened, she just smiled and said, 'You don't have to worry, as these people are your family who have gone into the spirit world. They come to talk to you because they love you'.

The penny dropped.

'You mean, ghosts?' I gulped.

'Yes, dear, but don't worry. You have more reason to fear the living than the dead.'

That was it for me! For many years I switched off my connection and refused to have anything to do with it until my time to re-connect was upon me.

My journey through life always lead me into roles of position, managing people and businesses the last corporate role before I took up my spiritual path was as a Development Manager with a large retail outlet, training people on how's and whys which helped me develop as a trainer, so I am aware that we all learn in different ways, some of us are pragmatic and like the hands on approach, some of us like to read and absorb the facts (Theorists) and like to be sure of that knowledge is retained before they begin, some of you only need guide lines, a little coaching here and there we are all different. Therefore I have put my skills as a trainer to good use in the book so I can reach out to as many of you as possible. The exercises are all practical, easily written and are followed by an spiritual attunemnet to enforce the learning's so it is a comprehensive teaching.

I used to be a little O.C.D. but I am aware that this was a family trait, ancestral DNA, but I have healed this area of my life and I am so much more laid back, as being O.C.D. can make you stressed and stress is not good for anyone. Therefore I always look for the logical approach so there will be no 'airy-fairy' instructions, only tried and trusted exercises and teaching.

However, I might add that I do actually believe in fairies as I have had the privilege of seeing one, and for me seeing is believing, but that is another story altogether and you will have to come back another time to hear that particular tale.

I have enjoyed a very good life with many wonderful moments, but in contrast I have also suffered significant loss and pain. In fact, the past five decades have been a roller coaster of emotional experiences. These I now realise should be viewed as pure joy, after all, life is a gift; a gift from the Great Spirit, and all my earthy experiences have helped me become the compassionate soul I am today.

Certainly this great variety of experiences has developed me as a person and I have experienced profound change. In the past (In what I like to call my corporate days) I used to be a very earth-bound person: a woman of determination, driven by success. I was materialistic, egotistical driven by success and power of position, until the day I was shaken to my very core and experienced an awakening of my soul. This experience was a meeting of such magnitude it was beyond anything from my limited comprehension of the universe.

As a being of spirit I had always been aware of the spirit world but chose to disregard it. As a consequence of my meeting with a being of light, an angel, something awoke within me. It was such a profound experience that almost instantaneously I became that person I would say

I am now: I have woken up from my sleep state. I am now, what some might choose to call, 'enlightened'.

That powerful and extraordinary moment of my 'awakening' shook me to a state of sublime consciousness and I found I could no longer ignore the true facts of my earthly journey; I was not here to acquire wealth and status but to acquire knowledge and grow my spirit. At that moment the course of my life changed forever.

I have always possessed the gift of mediumship and always managed to connect to the spirit world even though I did not know how I did it. To be quite honest it just happened! Even though I struggled with the concept and the notion of having mediumship abilities these connections occurred even though I didn't want them to!

It was only at the beginning of the new millennium that I allowed my spiritual light to shine, something that had always been there, woken by my pre-arranged meeting before I was born, because of my life lessons of how to deal with materialism, I am now in that enlighted place as a consequence of my angelic encounter.

I was a successful business woman after all, a high achiever, I thought I knew what I was doing, but as the years passed I found my success was not coupled with happiness and life appeared hollow. It is strange how synchronicities begin to happen, links are made and we are seemingly lead towards our destiny and this is exactly what happened to me.

My revelation, the change to my inner being, emanated from a meeting which transformed everything about me. Over a decade ago, I found myself in an unplanned meeting with a career advisor, I don't really know why I was there to be honest, it just happened. But this was no ordinary career advisor as he (I say he but he was male form but androgynous, no sex organs) was from the spirit world — "An Angel"— you can imagine my feelings at the time, it's almost impossible to describe accurately but I know this meeting was so profound it completely changed my life.

As a consequence of this powerful interaction, I now pen this book to help enlighten, encourage and advise you on your own journey of discovery.

"Without the spiritual world the material world is a disheartening enigma"
Joseph Joubert (1754 – 1824)

"Patience is the companion of wisdom".
Saint Augustine (354-430)

I think the thing I must impress on anyone reading this book is the need for patience. I do wonder why is it that when we decide we are going to learn something new, we suddenly develop impatience and see ourselves reaching our goal before we have taken the first step of our journey. This is so common and we really do need to guard against this tendency as it is extremely important.

I would like you to remember, learning to be a spiritual medium/psychic will be no different to anything else you have ever learned in your life. I thought I would use the metaphor of learning to drive so you can begin to understand the importance of achieving the fundamental elements right at the start of your literal and metaphorical journey.

Picture this; your first lesson has arrived. You walk to the car and sit in the driving seat, and place your hands on the steering wheel. You are so keen to get on the road that you want to miss out the instruction about the equipment and how it works.

The most important part of driving a car is to learn how it operates, how you start and stop safely. Mediumship is the exactly same.

It is important you can see in your rear-view mirror and know where the indicators are. Mediumship is the same. But you are too busy thinking of how long it will take you to pass your test, how many lessons you will need to pass, and all this before you have turned the key in the ignition. Mediumship is exactly the same. Would you ever think Oh I can drive, without a lesson and take a car out on the road alone without instruction or indeed, without passing your test, NO I didn't think so, so please bear that in mind and remember it is people lives you are dealing with when working with mediumship, exactly like driving a car without tuition.

The equipment and how it works is the most important part of driving, as it is with mediumship. First, you have to know how the car works, how you work.

Your tutor manages to attract your attention once more and, eventually, you listen to their instruction on pedals, indicators and adjusting your mirror.

The big moment arrives, you turn the key and the engine purrs. Your heart races with excitement and you are driving, a bit jumpy to start, but soon cruising smoothly along the road. Your instructor alerts you to your speed. Slow down; the lesson won't advance any quicker if you drive faster.

Mediumship is the same. You will not learn if you try to rush things. Indeed you will miss out fundamental elements that are of the utmost importance. Take it slowly at the start of your journey and get the foundations right so they are right for life. As you will already know It is harder to remove bad habits once they are installed (in all aspects of our lives), so learn the right way first; the basics. Do you understand what I have been trying to tell you? Patience is most definitely a virtue so learn it now!

It is not a race. Each person will learn at their own pace, in the time that is right for them This book gives a strong foundation on which to build your house of knowledge, and for those who have already started construction; sometimes it is good to return to basics and revise what you have achieved so far, remember you will always be learning on this journey it never stops as you evolve and learn so does your mediumship skills.

I would like to teach you the knowledge I have acquired from my group of workers in the spirit world, and from teachers here on the earth plane, regarding my journey of discovery. My aim is to teach you all I have learned from sitting in the power, which will give you a strong foundation on which to build your own development, now and in the future.

Remember, real growth comes with time, dedication, love:

The love of working with spirit;
The joy of feeling its unconditional love pour all around you, until your very essence is floating within it;
The love and wonder at this immense power, this magnificent universe.

The intellect of the spirit is great and tries to communicate with all who would listen. Open up your spirit and listen to what is whispered in the wind. Lift up your hearts, lift your mind and rejoice that you are mortal, that you are learning such wonderful lessons. As you are learning you are developing your soul".

"The reason birds can fly and we can't is simply that they have perfect faith, for to have faith is to have wings"
J. M. Barrie (1860 – 1937)

Intention

'Stop looking for the meaning of life and lead a meaningful Life.'
Simon G. James

The intention of this book is twofold, primarily it's a tutorial, regarding how to become a psychic and if you have the ability, a medium. This book is also a teaching manual with a series of tutorial exercises, guided meditations and is designed to be a practical working tool. It can be used to develop yourself alone if you cannot find an existing circle or group. It is a reference point, something you can use forever.

I will take you through a series of practical exercises to help you heighten the awareness of your intuition. I will also guide you towards different levels of awareness throughout the exercises. This is accompanied by a guided meditation or attunement at the end of each tutorial to help you on your journey of discovery.

To explain, an attunement is similar to meditation in that you are in an altered state of awareness, but always with one part of the mind alert, listening, sensing the communications from the spirit world. Each attunement will be related to previous exercises and every experience will be different.

We all have a team of spirit workers, I am not the exception and my main worker has been with me all of my life and has made his presence felt at times of need. He has a great sense of humour and the name he gave me for penning the book reflects this, Alchemeds. He was last here on earth around the 14th century and we have similar interests: divination, astrology and healing, he told me that we are part of a team, like the workings of a clock or watch, each cog within the mechanism needs the other to turn harmoniously and to be of benefit for each. This is a simple yet visionary explanation and typical of Alchemeds; you will get to know him a little more as you work through the book.

Where you are at this time whatever you are doing part of your life plan your destiny, it is meant to be, "It is written", what does that mean

"It is written" you may ask? Before you came to earth there were certain fundamental aspects of your life you agreed to and these agreements are kept or appears in the Akashi records, a record of what your life's purpose on this particular visit to the earth, a record of who, what, where and why you are here. We are all spirit and it is with blessings from the Great Spirit I bring you a book to help illuminate a path of spiritual growth; a journey of discovery and enlightenment.

Akashi is an ancient Sanskrit word meaning "hidden library", this secret hall of records can be revealed by connecting to your own spirit, unlocking the information from your soul. The information you will discover is your "destiny", your life's purpose, something we are all connected to in this vast universe. The Akashi is as real as you and I; it is a subatomic energy field and waves of information which are found within in all living things.

Its information, when accessed shows us we are all interconnected. Everything in this vast universe is connected with energy fields, the planets and the stars as well as each other as we are all energy vibrating at different frequencies and we can see clearly some of these effects in the way the moon pulls and creates tides and it affects us too as we are 80% water and we will all react differently during a full moon.

The reason you are investigating you spirit potential reading this book and others like it is that "it is written" you will awaken from your sleep of earthly materialistic ways and finally remember your soul is here for a purpose and you are more than just a physical body. Edgar Cayce an American trance medium was known for his work with the Akashic records, he was know as the sleeping prophet, he would lie down on his sofa, close his eyes and go into a sleep state and enter the hall of records, this is a quote from him.

"The records that have been written have been written.... That the natural question of the entity, from which has been given, is; From what sourse, or how, is such a record read of the activities in the past? How may self know that there is being given a TRYE record of the activities in a period of which there is no written word, of, history? Yet the entity itself sees and is being taught, and is studying the records that are written in nature, in the hills, in the rocks, in the trees, in that termed the genealogical log of nature itself. Just as true, then is the record that the mind makes upon the film of time and space in the activities of the body with its soul that is made in the image of the Maker; being then spirit in its form, upon the records IN time and space"

Revelation 20:12:
And I saw the dead, small and great, stand before God and the books were opened; and an other book was opened, which is the book of life: and the dead were judged out of those things which were written in the books, according to their works.

Mediumship is multi-faceted and is only one method of enlightenment. It is my chosen path before I came to the earth plane. For years I had pushed it away, frightened by what it might actually signify. But now here I am embracing it, encouraging its growth, so I can walk towards my purpose here on earth which is to use this gift as a healing tool, to heal the soul incarnate and discarnate. It is my intention to write these tutorials for individuals, to teach them how to connect and develop mediumship skills in a safe and grounded way.

My mission statement is "food for the soul" it couldn't be anything else for me, as I was born in May and my sign is ruled by Venus the Goddess of pleasure, a Tureen lady who has worked with food all of her life, that's me, so "food for the soul" had to my mission statement, there was no choice but it also hints at the business woman in me too! I am practical and this will keep me focused on my journey in assisting you.

There are many roads you can travel on through life and this applies when you awaken your spirit. Your soul within, will encourage you to seek and find where and what is right for you. This will happen when you listen to your soul and allow its light to shine. To awaken and follow your soul's purpose will ultimately spell out what spirituality actually means to you. This process will connect your and possibly the spirit world and ultimately to the Great Spirit: the universe.

The 'God force' knows us all, He alone knows all the answers, but as I write I would like to ask you to investigate what your soul is trying to tell you. What moves you? What makes you happy, makes you feel alive? This is an essential part of your journey, by beginning to direct yours thoughts inwardly, forgetting external forces and pressures that usually consume your thoughts, you can become to realise who you truly are.

Remember, it is no coincidence you are reading this book; it is certainly no mystery to spirit. Your souls growth and journey here on this visit to earth is written in the Akashi records, that you are spirit and are now beginning your own journey of mediumistic or spiritual discovery.

Through the teachings within the book I hope to inspire you to become ambassadors for the spirit world. It is my intention the book should be a working tool, giving you the understanding of how to connect to the world of spirit, and how to develop yourself for personal progression, or as a stepping stone on your journey of advancement towards working for spirit.

Once you undertake your journey it will inspire you to learn more about the world of spirit and perhaps, most importantly to understand and also use your psychic gifts. There will be pertinent moments of change within your life, as well as with your awareness of the spirit world. Listen to the small still voice within you, and then identify with your guides in your own personal way. I will show you how, the presentation and tutorial style, and meditations will inspire you on your awe-inspiring journey of discovery.

The more you work on the exercises, surrender all doubt and develop total trust in the spirit world, the greater your rewards will be and you will discover the profound evidence of survival will be revealed as you begin to connect to the spirit within and those around you. Connecting to spirit is and should be an enjoyable experience for everyone. One of the benefits of regularly sitting in the energy of spirit is you become more aware of the intelligence and personality of the people you are working with as they are the ones who will help you grow and connect to spirit. You will also come to know with one hundred percent certainty that life continues after death.

I hope you enjoy your journey and the inspiration this book will bring and its encouragement in allowing you to be all that you can be.

In The Beginning.......

I have had a few teachers over the years and I trust my spirit team implicitly. Sometimes the language deployed may appear harsh and direct, (remember the spirits come from a different time).

Within this book I wish to share information channelled through me by my guide who is assisting me as I write. His name is Alchemeds and he last lived on earth in the 14th century. Back then he was an Astrologer, herbalist, scientist and people came from far and wide to ask for his help and advice.

The following information I am writing is Alchemeds channelling through me!

"In the beginning it is important that you value the information you are being given by your tutor, as not only is it invaluable, but tutors possess experience and wisdom to share with you, and in most cases the spiritual worker/guide of the tutor has a great influence on what is being taught" (he laughs here as he likes this idea).

"Therefore, when you think you have already done a particular exercise, and think that you could miss one out, this is your first mistake, yes we all make mistakes, even me, here in the spirit world. (He laughs again)

This is not the correct decision, first and foremost on the earth plane everyone is in such a hurry, they want to finish before they get started, and secondly and most importantly, discipline is the most important and valued lesson in these tutorial sessions as each time you connect to a particular exercise with a specific goal in mind your spirit and your spirit team always have different ideas, (he laughs again) we know what you have to learn and that is always the important factor, I am working with your tutor to help you achieve the basics, a strong foundation upon which to build your house of knowledge. '

You may have done similar exercises with another tutor but it is not the same as doing it with the current one. In the first instance, the energy of each tutor is different as is the guidance from spirit. You should always look at all the exercises you do as a learning curve, a driving force, pushing you forward on your way to becoming an educator of spirit. Every time you learn, you are placing a piece of your spiritual body together, and it is not until all the pieces are in place that you can say, 'I am whole!'

One of the first things to consider in learning to be a spiritual being is to start by asking yourself what this actually means. By being aware of your spiritual body and beginning to take note that a spiritual journey means you are putting yourself into service for others, always helping your fellow man.

Remember:

- Compassion and Empathy
- Being Loving and Giving

These are wonderful stepping stones for your spiritual growth, so my friends, I would say to you, first look at yourself, what kind of person are you?

- Do people approach you with their problems?
- Do you listen?
- Are you sympathetic to great injustices in your world?
- Do you try to look after your planet and do what you can to preserve her?
- First and foremost on your journey, do you know who you are?

With pureness in your heart you will not only be developing a skill, you will be developing your spirit; the very essence of the god force within you.

So take the time to heed my statement before you head off on your quest for development!

You may be a medium, you may be psychic but you are most definitely spirit within a physical body. Therefore it is essential that you now accept who you are, as you are.

You are a beautiful soul on this earth, which is a gift from the Great Spirit, given so that you can use your skills wisely and keep learning but, most of all:

love yourself and treat your brethren as you would wish to be treated.

However, the greatest thing I can tell you is to have fun. Enjoy your life as no matter how many years you will dwell on the earth plane, it is but a short space in time and you will return home to the (spirit world) too soon.

It should be with a sense of completion, knowing you did everything you intended to do, you lived a full and happy life" end of channeling.

I am already half a century and it has flown by so quickly, now I live my life with gusto and in the principles of a spiritual awareness so enjoy your time while on the earth plane.

Channelling Begins:- The Physical Body

"What about your physical body? Do you know how it works? Most people have no real idea and do not wish to know. Many folk have no interest in the mechanics of how or what their body is doing. They are happy to get up every morning wash, feed and go about their daily lives. Let me tell you now, your physical body has a significant impact on your spiritual work and therefore it is important to start listening, exploring and paying attention to what your body is telling you.

When you begin your path of enlightenment you will become increasingly sensitive and your physical body will become more sensitive too. Try to listen to what your body tells you when it needs nourishment, if we only take time to listen it will tell us what we need. Eat only naturally grown products, try to avoid chemical-filled foods as they will cause illness as you evolve. Some of your bodies need meat, so again listen to your intuition. Eat foods in season and local to your area too. All these considerations are as important to your journey as exercise and taking sufficient rest. If the body is in good working order connecting to the spirit world will be little easier.

Never take your spiritual body for granted: teach it, cherish it, love and develop it, and you will see it blossom and grow strong".

"Earthlings have such a need for wealth; it is like a disease, a hunger.

My friends, I can tell you this; all the gold in the world will not get you into the house of our Father. Your material wealth is an illusion you cannot take it with you, only love is real! By growing your spirit and living a spiritual life, you will have wealth so great that your spiritual being, your inner house, will be filled with gold.

As a being of inter-dimensions (spirit), I know you do not need an elixir to prolong life, as I know life is eternal. Only the physical body dies; the heavy coat that our spirit body carries while we are here on the earth plane diminishes after time. So I encourage you all to become alchemists: go and fill your life with golden acts of kindness, and go in the knowledge that you will live forever, as the spirit never dies".

End of Channelling .

Note:
The word 'alchemy' as defined in the Collins Compact Dictionary:

'A medieval form of chemistry concerned with trying to change base metals into gold, and to find an elixir to prolong life indefinitely'.

AURA

Before we begin to explore the realms of those worlds that intermingle with our own we need to understand some fundamentals. As with all teachings it is important to give those studying a foundation from which to learn. We will start with the first spiritual part of our bodies, which can be seen (by some) with the spiritual eye; the bio-magnetic field also known as the Aura.

Every living thing has an aura; a subtle energy that surrounds us. Our aura is an energetic extension of our physical bodies; an energy field which holds all the information about us within it. Everything on this planet is made of matter. Matter can take three forms - solid, liquid or gas. All matter is made up of atoms. It is a subatomic energy field of quantum particles and waves of information which are found within all living things, we are all energy vibrating at different frequencies, which give off different colours. Scientists are now very much aware of this and even study it in quantum physics.

Different objects are made up of different types of atoms. Inside each atom, there is a nucleus. Orbiting the nucleus are electrons. The energy of the orbiting electrons produces heat, which causes the electrons to gain energy. When electrons gain energy, they move out further from the nucleus of the atom. When the electrons cool down and return to normal orbit, the energy is released in the form of light (called a photon).So heat energizes the atoms to produce light.

The colour of the light depends on the amount of energy released by the atom. Colour is measured by frequency. High frequency light has high energy and low frequency light has low energy. Of the visible colours, red has the lowest frequency and violet has the highest frequency. So the energy produced by the atom determines the frequency of the light wave, which is interpreted by the eye as colour.

We humans are made up of atoms as well. Our atoms produce energy, which produce photons. The colour of your skin, eyes and hair are all interpreted by the eye using the photons our atoms produce.

If you put the palms of your hands close together, you will feel warmth. This warmth is the energy produced by the atoms in your body. This is your aura. Eyes that are trained to work in partnership with intuition can see the different frequencies of light, or colour, between the palms.

The Human aura is also associated with feelings, clairsentence. Positive feelings generally create bright colours, whereas negative feelings generally create dark colours. Problems in the aura will eventually lead to problems in the first and third layers, causing physical or mental illness.

The etheric Human aura extends about two inches out from the physical body and is usually a shade of whitish blue in colour. The shade of the blue relates to the physical condition and health of the Human physical body. Athletes have strong etheric auras of a deeper blue in shade. In the etheric (Human aura) you feel all the sensations, both painful and pleasurable. Whenever there is pain the flow of energy in that area of the etheric is erratic.

Draw a circle on your left hand using your right fingertip. Don`t let your finger touch your hand and keep it at a distance of about a half inch. Move slowly. You will feel the power of your aura.

Everybody has the ability to see (psychically) the Human aura, it is just a matter of training your eyes to look beyond the physical. For beginners a low light is the best way to start. Turn out the lights and lie on your bed, or sit comfortably on a chair. As you are lying on the bed hold your hands out at full distance in front of you. Don`t stare hard but rather just gaze at your hands, similar to looking at a 3d image, look beyond it. Moving your hands slowly, bring your fingertips together until they are almost touching. You will notice a cloudy blue haze appear around your finger. This is the etheric Human aura.

The ketheric template layer (also known as your aura) extends about thirty six to forty eight inches from the physical body and appears as an extremely bright golden light that is rapidly pulsating. This layer takes on the form of a golden egg that surrounds and protects everything within it.

The mental layer extends about four to eight inches from the physical body and is usually a bright shade of yellow. Within this layer are our thoughts and mental processes. The more active our thinking processes the brighter our mental layer becomes.

Each layer represents a different energy, each generally finer than the last layer, and each vibrating at a higher frequency than the previous one. Although layers may appear to be separate from one another, they will overlap the layers beneath them.

Kirilian photography can capture the aura, and if you know where you can have a photograph of your aura taken, then do so. You will find that it will be different each time it is taken, as your aura changes with your mood and development.

So why do we need to know about the aura? The aura is the tool you use to help you become more intuitive, you have probably used it a thousand times without realising. Your aura can intermingle with other people's auras and when this happens you unconsciously read from their bio magnetic field and you may pick up disturbances within it like physical ailments. You may suddenly get a headache, which is not your own but the person you are talking to; you are picking up that information from their aura. You may also pick up if the person is feeling happy or sad. We sometimes actually refer to people we meet with phrases such as: "you look bright and cheery today" or "you feel a little blue" are you ok?" You are subconsciously picking it up from there aura!

The Aura stores every piece of information about you from birth and when you work on a psychic link with someone as we have just discussed you are reading the bio magnetic field. So when you are more conscious that you can do this and become aware of when people come into your "space" or aura, you are sensitising your aura to begin to pick up other peoples energy fields.

You will also notice that some people seem to leave you feeling tired after being in their company. This is because they are drawing energy from your aura, so it is important to be aware of this. By monitoring how other auras and your own are throughout the day, consciously at first, you are helping to grow your intuition. Being more aware of your aura will help you strengthen it and if you are aware of people who take your energy you can protect yourself by imagining mirrors around you and this enables their energy hooks to bounce right back at them. This is only one method and further strategies are discussed later in the book.

Your aura has seven layers, which are:

- Etheric body
- Physical body
- Emotional body
- Mental body
- Spiritual body
- Astral layer
- Ketheric template

"A healthy body is the guest chamber of the soul"
Francis Bacon (1561- 1626)

Angel Anne says:

I remember when I was first developing, people talked of the aura and how important is was, at that time I didn't quite understand how important it actually was and I found it all confusing if I am honest.

Now I understand the aura stores all information incarnate or discarnate (alive or in spirit world)

It holds our potential for the future: our dreams and aspirations

Injuries and illness are shown in the aura,

The colours themselves are ever changing and a book could be written on this subject alone.

Everything is energy, everything has a life force and you can tell so much by simply looking at the aura, just the other day my sister came for a visit and I had not seen her for about ten days as I had been away.

She had just come down the stairs from having said good night to my grandchildren who were sleeping over that evening. As she stood at the bottom of my stairs I could see a her aura, lots of green all around he face on the physical layer, oh I thought looks like she is in quite a bit of pain, I could also see yellow to her centre and right hand side as well as the energy of a young man behind her in spirit, I knew he was in spirit and not the energy of her son here on the earth plane as the colours are more iridescent almost pearlised just like the sheen from a pearl.

So I said why are you worried about your health? You seem to be receiving healing around your face are you in pain, "I am a little worried, I was at the doctors yesterday" she said, "I have discomfort and pain in my breasts and I had an intense treatment today on my face which was very painful as the numbing cream did not work". I understood all this in a moment just by looking at her aura, now her son here has a twin in the spirit world and I never give her any information on him as I feel she thinks I am trying to make her "feel better"!

So I said to her, close your eyes for a moment and try to feel with your aura to your right but bearing in mind it is slightly behind you. Do you feel anything?' I asked., "why yes' she said, ' there is a coolness but a warmth with it slightly above me and it feels as if it is linking with me in some way", I told her to take a breath and get a feeling of who this could be she smiled and then tears fell from her eyes. "it's Lewis" (her son), 'Yes' I said, "How did you do that?", she exclaimed.

'I didn't' I said, 'you did it. Really it is that easy.' You see our aura is so sensitive and when we learn how we feel as people or become aware of our own energies we learn to detect other people's energies when we quieten our minds and become aware of our aura, we can feel, sense it, know it, so this is a big part of your development. It is such an important but exciting aspect of the whole process and when I realised this, I too suddenly knew just how important the aura actually is.

"The human body is vapour, materialised by sunshine and mixed with the life of the stars"
Paracelsus (1493-1541)

Sensing the colour of the aura should be spontaneous, we are all light beings, multi-dimensional and each of us unique which as I explained earlier vibrate different colours, so we are each a colour and different shades and varieties of each colour, there is a saying in Ireland "fifty shades of green" which could be from apple green, mint green, forest green to emerald green, how many of you have gone to a DIY store to purchase some paint and thought, that is the colour I need, and when you get home it is way off? Our perception of the colour was different from the reality and as each of us has a different perception of what a colour is, therefore each opinion will be different from another's, so, it is important that we analyse colour for ourselves as we each perceive it to be different, there are people who suffer from colour blindness and how they perceive colour will be entirely different from those who are not, if we go back in time to the cave man his eye sight was only advanced enough to pick up dark and light and as we evolved through the ages we began to become aware of different colours.

In the Bible book of Isaiah 1.18 it reads:

"Come now, let us reason together, says the Lord: though your sins are like scarlet, they shall be as white as snow; though they are red like crimson, they shall become like wool".

Which lets us see that man can now perceive more colour as he evolved through the ages, however the bible also quote's the three colours of the rainbow, red, yellow and green, mankind's evolvement was not enough at that time to see the higher vibrational colours of blue and violets, so as we evolve we are aware of colour through our own perception which is what each of us has to do, even though I will give you the most commonly known meanings for colour it is important that you gather your own book of perception and meaning for your own development. It is important to stick to your perception of a particular colour, and this will prove vital to your development as a psychic or medium, as you evolve your own abilities to interpret colour. When we look at the Renaissance period we can clearly see that many of the artist of that time were working in the altered state as we can see they were able to see the auric field which is pictured as a halo around the figures within their work and it is so with so many of the great musicians of yesteryear and today they move into the altered state and can see the aura or hear inspiration from the spirit. Today we have a young girl, Akiane Kramarik who's is inspired by spirit she believe she paints through god her work is amazing and you can see she is clearly linked to the higher world of spirit.

So as we evolve the colours of your aura will also change, our emotional body as it suggests is all about how we have lived the feelings of how life has affected us the good the bad and indifferent, our joys and illness all stored within the physical body and it is possible to give an account of someone's medical history from within the auric field, so you will find as a consequence of moods, health and general wellbeing that the colour will vary. The colour of the light depends on the amount of energy released by the atom. Colour is measured by frequency. High frequency light has high energy and violet has the highest frequency. So the energy produced by the atom determines the frequency of the light wave. As you develop you will inevitable realise you have someone from spirit helping you with this evolvement and when spirit impresses on our nervous system when we enter spiritual space as it were there is no time or conception of time just space we become "one" part of that consciousness there is really no separation, when we think of spirit they are instantly there, when we send up out thoughts they see them, so be mindful of your thoughts as thought are things and manifest!

The following is a very brief outline of colours and their common interpretation. The following are to be used as a rough guide only, as you should always follow your feelings and trust your instincts.

"Vision is the art of seeing what is invisible to others"
Jonathon Swift (1667-1745)

The Meaning of Colours in the Aura

Aqua & pale blues: high communications, the colour of sensitivity, strong natural instincts.

Dark Blue: intuition coming from the higher dimensions of the aura represents harmony, people who have found their chosen path in life, mediumship, and strong ethics.

Turquoise: creative, struggled to achieve, honesty

Indigo: strong psychic ability.

Amber: personal strength and courage, in people who are going through positive career changes, period of problems is coming to an end.

Mushroom/light browns: a slowing of destiny, a hard worker, people who challenge convention.

Dark Browns: indicates a person with common sense.

Gold: a higher level of consciousness.

Pale Greens: spiritual advancement, healers, friendly, sometimes economical with the truth.

Jade/dark Green: charitable nature, emotional and mental stress, scrooge, jealousy.

Grey: people who feel trapped in life, depression.

Apricot: Humanitarian, healer, caring.

Orange: healer, good health, strong motivation, self-control.

Pale pink: true love, loyalty and commitment, people who work in a career they love

Pink: sexual desire.

Dusty pink: foolish people.

Lilac: spiritual balance, I have often seen this in people who have had a near death experience.

Magenta: often found in entrepreneurs, humble people, and laziness.

Dark Red: short tempered, found in people with a big ego.

Bright Red: physical mediumship,natural creative skills, self-empowerment, self-determination.

Silver: this is the link between the spiritual realm.

Pale yellows: shyness, optimism, strength of direction

Golden yellows: teachers, inspiration, day dreamers sometimes manipulators.

White: indicates purity and or protection, and spirit workers within the aura itself.

When reading auras it is vital you look at the colours connecting to each other and what the combination of those colour mean so that a true reading can be given. It is also important you trust your intuition.

As well as learning about the colours in your aura, you can learn how to see auras. You may or may not see them at the moment, but your psychic gifts can develop and this will enable you to see more.

I find it very easy to see auras if I am looking at a person with a blank wall behind them, preferably a light-coloured wall. Try asking a friend to do this for you. As they are standing there, look past them at the top of the head or shoulder area. Relax your eyes, look at the top of the head, but past it, like looking at a 3-D picture. You will see a whitish blue colour first and, over time you will begin to see other colours too.

"What Lies behind us and what lies before us are tiny matters compared to what lies within us"
Ralph Waldo Emerson (1803 – 1882)

Chakras

The energy system of our bodies is far more complex than you might think. In addition to the seven layers of our auric field, we have hundreds of chakras and meridians throughout our body. The chakras connect our bio-magnetic field (aura) and our physical bodies and act, among other things, as a linkage point to higher consciousness and spiritual beings.

These energy centres function as pumps, regulating the flow of energy throughout our energy field, filtering information back to the physical body. The functioning of the Chakras can reflect how we choose and make decisions even though the Chakras are not part of our physical body. They are actually denser than the aura and act as a shield for the vital organs which lie behind each of the seven main Chakras. They interact with our physical bodies through the endocrine and nervous systems.

All of your senses and states of awareness are filtered and felt through the Chakras, any tension, physical or emotional within your being is felt within the Chakra in the first instance. We all have a sensitive area or weak area of the physical body, the associated Chakra in conjunction with this area will be the first point to feel stress and will be held here. As a consequence it will have an effect on the organs associated with it, therefore if stress continues over a long period of time the person will inevitable produce physical symptoms within the body itself.

It is important therefore to regularly check your spiritual body and keep it clear of stress before it manifests as illness within the physical being, one way to do this is by regularly cleansing your aura through meditation and visualisation exercises which are included in your download or by receiving Reiki healing, an energetic system of healing the aura and chakras to help prevent physical ailments.

The Chakras have a physical effect on your body, however like the breath the chakras work subconsciously continuing to move and spin without us needing to remind ourselves to do this, so no real thought is needed to help with their natural function, but at times they can become "blocked" or feel out of tune or alignment, as illness starts in the aura and moves through to the chakras before entering the physical body, so we can pick up, energetically a problem within the chakra, wither or not that means the chakra is out or it is the illness that is affecting our senses it does appear in the chakra and as each major chakra protects vital organs behind them, it is important to address the un-balance.

The Chakras have invoked great discussions and interests in energetic healing systems, we now have vast teachings in our western world on the chakras and these teachings lead us to believe the chakras are one colour but if we look at the teachings given to us by the ancient civilisation of India and Tibet they teach that the chakras have one predominant colour but usually at least two others, Charles Leadbetter has written some great books on the subject and his knowledge is greater than mine so I would suggest you read his book.

I do know that our chakra's are an energy exchange system that draw in light form the universe and then is projected back it is about balancing the body, giving and receiving.

The word 'Chakra' is an ancient Sanskrit word meaning 'wheel'. The concept of the Chakra dates back to 2000 BC and is found in the ancient Hindu texts "The Vedas". While chakra traditions and teachings are varied and often contradictory, they have certainly inspired remarkable passions and teachings and are referred to in most energy healing work.

The chakra is a wheel-like spinning vortex forming a specific layer of the auric field. The whirling circular motion forms a cavity, or vacuum, in the centre that draws in anything it encounters on its particular vibrational level. This is then processed and returned to the auric field. The chakras are a protection for the internal organs.

As a psychic medium, who is profoundly clairsentient I work on feeling (aura), which is the solar plexus chakra, the upper stomach and all information comes through that chakra. And as a multi dimensional being as we all are and all of us vibrate at different frequencies, therefore I will like and will be drawn to some people's vibrations because they are on a similar wave length to mine,(Like attracts like) and possibly higher as we are drawn in by spiritual and healing vibrations of others as we work with our energy systems . So if we work on the law of attraction, the opposite can be said for those I am not attracted to, there are some energies I would rather avoid, some I really don't like and some can actually make me feel nauseous.

Whatever the effect might actually be all the information flows in through the aura into my chakra. It is then processed and returns to my chakra and I physically process it as information.

I vibrate yellow as I have many auric photographs taken and surprisingly (or not) my solar plexus or stomach is very sensitive, It has always been this way, I have to watch what I eat and any illness usually generate tummy problems, even a cold! I am aware of this so I can help my sensitive area by watching what foods that I eat the company I keep and generally give healing to this sensitive area, It is no surprise that I vibrate as yellow as It is the colour of teaching and learning two things I have being doing all my life, (my mother said I have been bossing her around from the age of two).

The more you work with spirit the more sensitive you become, so you have to develop and acute awareness of your chakras as all illness begins in the aura, progresses to the chakra then into the physical resulting in physical illness. If you become aware of this you will know instinctively when your body is out of synch and can rectify it before it manifests itself as a physical illness

The seven major chakras of the human body are aligned along the spinal column, and are at the front and back of the body.

- The Crown Chakra
- The Brow Chakra
- The Throat Chakra
- The Heart Chakra
- The Solar Plexus (upper stomach)
- The Sacral Chakra (lower stomach)
- The Root Chakra

There are twenty-one minor chakras, or secondary chakras. Most of these are located in the trunk of the body, but also are found in the palms of the hands, the soles of the feet and the major joints of the arms and legs.

Each chakra regulates a specific area of the physical and emotional body. When a chakra spins perfectly with no obstructions or sluggishness, it is functioning well and will not cause any problems physically, mentally or emotionally within its regulated area.

In any study of the anatomy of the aura it is important to understand the significance of the chakra system. The chakras exist on all levels of the aura and serves as linking mechanisms between the auric field and the physical body, as well as linking mechanisms between the different levels of the auric field itself.

It is usually believed the three lower chakras correlate to the basic primary needs:

survival, protection and will

Whereas, the four higher chakras are concerned with our psychological make-up, defining love, communication, knowledge and connection with the spirit world.

While there are many energy and meridian centres within the body, I am only concerned with showing you the major chakras, as well as the name and purpose of each.

The chakras influence your physical body as well as your spiritual body. If a chakra is out of balance then the body part related to that particular chakra may be out of balance.

First Chakra

The Base sometimes known as The Root Chakra: or Muladahara

is situated at the base of the spine and the pubic bone.

Its colour is red; its element is earth and vibrates to the musical note C

Its time of development is between birth and five years.

Its associated area of consciousness is the physical body, which includes all physical sensations, pain, power, pleasure and to our survival instincts and a positive self-image. It governs our perception of the physical world, willpower, motivation and intent and assists in our ability to remain grounded.

The physical organ association for this chakra includes the gonads, the glomus, coccygeum, the adrenal gland, the kidneys and the spinal column. If this becomes blocked this blockage can manifest itself as paranoia, insecurity, a feeling of being out of touch with gravity, fertility issues, and low libido.. Crystals may be used to help keep this Chakra in balance such as Smoky Quartz, Garnet, Alexandrite, Ruby, Agate, Bloodstone, Onyx, Tiger's Eye and Obsidian.

Second Chakra

Here we encounter change.

The Sacral Chakra or Swadhisthana

Is situated behind, or just below, the navel.

Its colour is orange and its element is water and vibrates to the musical note of D

Its time of development is between three and eight years old

The area of consciousness it governs is emotion. This includes our sexuality and awareness of others, and governs feelings. The quantity of sexual energy and vitality, security, creativity, and sincerity we experience emanates here. If the second chakra becomes blocked it can manifest this by producing emotional problems, sexual guilt, lust, and base emotions issues.

Its physical organ association includes the spleen, kidneys and the bladder, lymphatic.

Some crystals that can be used to help keep this Chakra in balance are Amber, Citrine, Topaz, Aventurine, Moonstone and Jasper.

Third Chakra

The Navel or Solar Plexus Chakra or Manipur known as the psychic pump, your gut instincts is situated in the upper stomach, just behind the rib cage. Its colour is yellow and its element fire and vibrates to the musical note E. Its time of development is between eight and twelve years old.

The area of consciousness it affects is the mental or intellectual body. It governs issues of personal power as well as emotional issues. The physical organ associated, includes the adrenal glands, the pancreas, the liver and the stomach and gives us a sense of our personal power in the world (willpower). It also relates to destiny, psychic ability, determination, assertion, personal power, and purpose. If blocked it can manifest itself in feelings, or as a sense of victimization, an inability to tackle issues, there is a danger of being overemotional and too attached to the idea of love, or possibly a fear of being alone. Some crystals that can be used to help keep this Chakra in balance are Yellow Citrine, Apatite, Calcite, Kunzite, Rose Quartz, Iron Pyrites (Fool's Gold) and Topaz. As before

Fourth Chakra

The fourth chakra integrates balance into the physical body and to our spirit mind this is the Heart Chakra or Anahata

The heart chakra is situated midway between the shoulder blades or between the breast bone. Its colour is green and its element is air and vibrates to the musical note F. Its time of development is between twelve and sixteen years old It is the area of consciousness: the astral body, which gives us the ability to bring and gives us the ability to express love for ourselves and others. It is also related to compassion and intuition

Its physical organ association is with the thymus gland, heart, blood and circulatory system, as well as the immune and the endocrine systems. If blocked it may manifest itself as a weak immune system or heart problems or a lack of compassion, a suppression of love towards others and self. If love is felt it will only be for a short time before it is withdrawn. Fear and rage can also accumulate and cause a block to this area and associated with this block is a feeling of being unworthy, self-pitying, and fear of rejection.

Some crystals that can be used to help keep this Chakra in balance are Emerald, Green Calcite, Amber, Azurite, Chrysoberyl, Jade, Rose and Watermelon Tourmalines.

Fifth Chakra

Here we enter the realm of consciousness where communication occurs, whether within ourselves or to and from another

The Throat chakra or Vishuddha.

Is situated in the throat area,

Its colour is blue and its element is sound and vibrates to the musical not of G.

The time of development is between sixteen and twenty-one years old.

The area of consciousness is the etheric body, which is a template for the physical body and represents our potential for perfection.

The physical organ association includes the thyroid and parathyroid glands, the lungs, vocal cords and bronchial apparatus. If this becomes blocked it can manifest itself in problems like laryngitis or sore throats, creative blocks, or general problems communicating with others, rigidity, prejudice, and an inability to accept other people's views. Some crystals that can be used to help keep this Chakra in balance are Lapis Lazuli, Aquamarine, Sodalite, Turquoise and Sapphire.

Sixth Chakra

The essence and function of this chakra is to 'see', in the sense we must accept that complete vision will include both darkness and light.

The Brow Chakra sometimes known as The Third Eye Chakra or Ajna.

It is situated in the centre of the head between the eyebrows.

Its colour is indigo and its element is light and vibrates to the musical note A

Time of development is between the age of twenty-one and twenty-six years.

The area of consciousness is the celestial body. It is here we have 'sixth sight' clairvoyance. We use this chakra to visualize.

Physical organ association with the sixth chakra is the pineal gland. If it becomes blocked it can manifest itself as sinus or eye problems, a wish to control others, egotism. Some crystals that can be used to help keep this

Chakra in balance are Amethyst, Purple Apatite, Azurite, Calcite, Pearl, Sapphire, Blue and White Fluorite.

Seventh Chakra

This represents our belief system, both conscious and unconscious.

The Crown Chakra or Sahasrara

is situated at the top of the head.

Its colour is white and its element is thought and vibrates to the musical note B.

Time of development is after the age of twenty-six years.

The area of consciousness is the 'ketheric', the spiritual realm, where we merge with God; the All that is.

Physical organ association is the pituitary gland. If blocked it can manifest itself as psychological problems, a feeling of alienation from others, and condemnation. Some crystals that can help keep this Chakra in balance are Diamond, White Tourmaline, White Jade, Snowy Quartz and Celestite.

How your aura connects to spirit,

I just want to give you a little explanation of how your aura is used in connecting to spirit.

Imagine this, you are the centre piece. On one side of you there is your emotional body, at the other is the mental body and at the back of you is your spirit body. Therefore three bodies are around you. To connect to spirit you first have to set the intention through your own spirit. Then send the intention into your emotional body (the feeling centre) and then into the mental body. When this attunement is happening, the energy, your vibration, is increasing and spirit can see this like a light, your light, so a passing spirit can recognise this and come forward for a communication. Now another person has entered the equation. Behind your spirit is the spirit communicator who now has to try to match your vibration by lowering theirs. They can now begin to communicate with your spirit.

Your spirit then moves into the emotional and mental bodies and once it is processed from the mental body it is processed by the physical body in the form of verbal communication. It is only when you begin to understand these faculties of mediumship that you can truly be aware that the aura is of the upmost importance and this facility, in my opinion, should be studied to your full potential.

Example of Blocked Chakra:

If your brow or throat chakra is out of balance:

Any chakra that is blocked will affect your aura and leave it vulnerable to outside influences. When working spiritually it is important to have balance between the throat and brow as these Chakras work on both mental and intuitive levels and are involved in communicating intuition, therefore it is important the throat or voice can communicate clearly what the inner eye is seeing or what is termed, ' the brow chakra'. Strong beliefs can block these Chakras, a blocked throat results in communication difficulties, problems can also arise if you feel suppressed by people around you and your fear of voicing your intuitive feelings, which in turn can block your brow chakra. The opposite can happen if your brow chakra is left to open then you may feel vulnerable to other people's thoughts and emotions and your psychic abilities will be hampered.

How can you prevent blockages or unbalance in the Chakras?

Again the only way to do this is to become familiar with your Chakras and by monitoring them regularly. You can do daily or weekly exercises to help you maintain a clear aura and functional chakras, you can scan your body from the top of your head and work your way down to the root Chakra.

Just imagine each Chakra spinning clock wise and then see or imagine it the right colour and size for you, as you are a living breathing being your Chakras should be too and not closed over as some people would have you believe, then do the same to all the chakras and work your way down the body this scan should only take you a few minutes when you reach the base chakra then imagine roots coming from your feet and push them deep into the earth imagine your roots are wet so they stick to the earth, now you are grounded and closed.

If this is difficult to imagine or you find it difficult to talk yourself through this process, then don't worry, there is a down load with the book and all the exercises to follow the practical lesson are included, so listen to track one on the down load.

PLEASE FOLLOW THE LINK FOR YOUR FREE DOWNLOAD TO THE ATTUNEMENTS. www.angelanne.co.uk/book/downloads

Listen to track one: Balancing the Chakras and Cleansing your Aura.

Use the page below to keep a record of how you felt during the attunement and each time you listen to it as it is a record of your development.

Now that you know a little about the aura and the chakras and how they work, let's move on to the next stage.

"The soul stirs within its chrysalis, dreaming that it will one day be an angel. It will."
Lou Andréas-Salome (1861- 1937)

Altered States of Awareness

Humans have always known how to enter different states of consciousness. Some do it by introducing hallucinogenic substances, some by chanting, fasting or by engaging in rituals that help them out of their normal state of being into an altered state of consciousness.

It is a well-known fact that certain religious orders for example, nuns, monks or Buddhists rise early in the morning and spend time praying and meditating. One of the reasons for this early morning ritual, which connects you inwards, is that your brain waves naturally omit alpha waves first thing in the morning. They are relaxed after waking from sleep, so it makes good sense to use this time to meditate and go within; to take your mind and body into a state of relaxation and to stay consciously aware of your surroundings.

Meditation relaxes you which, in turn, increases your vibration through that relaxed state into the alpha state. This alters your conscious levels, where intuition and inspiration, clairvoyance and much more, come into play.

Meditation fulfils many functions. It is an excellent way to relax, and helps reduce blood pressure, anxiety and also allows you to centre yourself, so is beneficial for your health.

The other great thing about meditating is that you can do it anywhere, at any time of the day. If you feel stressed or are losing control you can excuse yourself, take time out, and go within; go into a meditative state.

Relax yourself. This will help you see things more clearly and gives you focus again, without stress. You can meditate in any position, so people don't have to know you are meditating. You don't need to be in the lotus position on the floor, you can be sitting at your desk at work, outside on a bench or standing looking into space, or just going for a quiet walk, stilling the mind. All you have to ensure is that you are comfortable. If you are sitting down make sure you're in a position so that your joints don't go to sleep, or develop pins and needles.

Different Levels of Consciousness

- Beta state is fully awake. 14–30 brain waves per second.
- Alpha state is internal focus. 8–13 brain waves per second.
- Theta state is a deeper, altered state of consciousness; trance state. 4–7 brain waves per second.
- Delta state is deep sleep. Fewer than 4 brain waves per second.

Many of you may find that, when you first try to get into the altered state of consciousness, or the Alpha state, your brain tries to kick in with thoughts. Don't worry too much at this stage in your development, as it will take time to train the mind to be quiet, and it will not happen overnight. Be aware of any thoughts and then just let them go. Then focus within again, allowing the mind to relax in the alpha level of consciousness and you will find that your intuition increases after a period of time. Visions or clairvoyance will come into your mind's eye, and possibly spiritual connections, family, friends loved ones. Thoughts will flow into your mind, as working with the spirit world is a mind-to-mind communication.

There are many different forms of meditation:

Focused meditation is when you focus on an object. A candle flame is popular as you will find that over a period your eyes may become heavy and close.

Visualization meditations are very popular; that is, when a teacher talks you through a journey and you visualize your journey as they talk you through it.

Guided meditation is when you listen to pre-recorded tapes or CDs.

There are many different ways to meditate and it is best that you experiment and find your own way, as we are all unique.

I enjoy meditating on my own in nature, next to water if possible in a fairly quiet spot, but it is important to remember your personal safety: always use common sense and stay safe.

I have had some really powerful connections in meditations when sitting in a group. Therefore I suggest that whenever practically possible try to meditate with other people as the energy is stronger. That way you can build up confidence and discipline.

Personally there is more challenge when I sit in group situations as I try harder to connect to spirit. This is because I sense there may be a need for someone to receive a communication. As a consequence I always push my own boundaries so my mediumship does not become repetitive, and a training group is the perfect place to hone your skills

Many people find when they are drifting off to sleep (theta state) that people who have passed suddenly pop into their head. This is not by chance. Your mind or brain waves are reducing from beta state to alpha state, and your focus is going lower into the deeper levels of theta. At that stage, you may well sense those who are in the spirit realms, or you may get a great idea as your mind is shutting out the chatter and drifting downwards, focusing within.

Linking with the spirit world is a state of mind; you need a motive, a reason and a purpose, goal or aim. Where do you want to go with your mediumship?

Your conscious mind is the memory bank that spirit will use to acquire information. In the same way as a search engine does or your computer to find recently used files, spirit will use situation and scenarios from your life, taken from your cellular memory so that they can communicate with family and friends via this information. That is why most mediums have had varied and somewhat difficult life, as these experiences serve as stepping stones to growth emotionally and physically so they have empathy and understanding for many different people and perspectives.

Their purpose as teachers and healers is to communicate what they are being given or brought to the forefront of their minds with empathy and understanding for the recipient, as well as for the spirit world.

The subconscious mind carries out habitual behaviour: blinking, breathing and circulating the blood is done without thought. As your mediumship develops, your communication will be without thought; you will no longer allow your mind to take control, and will trust what you are receiving is coming from the spirit world. The subconscious is the imagination, if you like, as it is the imaginary part of your brain in which spirit creates pictures and clairvoyance.

Therefore, to become a medium you must focus on your development; your goal in life. It is not for the faint-hearted as you will not develop overnight. It is not a pastime (said from one who is serious about her work) it can be if you wish it to be however. I sometimes need to remember the spirit world wants to have fun too!

For me it is a vocation. I love my job and it is important to remember why we were drawn to spiritualism in the first place. There has to be a need to help it should come from a place of "service"; it is a joy to work for spirit but the greatest joy for me when I see spirit touching your spirit. Nothing is better, nothing beats that feeling of a soul connecting to another and the effect will leave a life-long impression.

As tennis players and concert pianists practise their skills to enhance and perfect them, so must a medium practise, practise, practise, to become finely tuned into the vibration of the spirit world.

It takes many years to reach the top of your game, no matter whether you are footballer, diver, musician or medium. Malcolm Gladwell states in his book, Outliers: The Story of Success (Little Brown 2008) that the key to success in absolutely anything is linked to the '10,000 Hour Rule'. This means any individual should practice whatever they want to master for around 10,000 hours. Which may well be worth bearing in mind. Certainly a constant need to fine tune and polish your development is a must to continue to grow and learn. You will give your best mediumship or connection to spirit just before entering the spirit world, how ironic!

The other thing to remember as you learn and grow with your development your opinions and knowledge change and increase. If someone had asked me two years ago if spirit grew up on the other side I would have said NO! As all my loved ones always showed me themselves exactly as they were before.

That was until my grandson died at two days old leaving his twin brother here on the earth to learn and grow. He has come to see me on many occasions.

The first I remember powerfully as it was furthest thing from my mind. While I was sitting in the power, it had been my intention to sit in a healing balm from spirit to bring in serenity for myself and as I was nearing the end of my time in the power. I heard footsteps and looked into my inner sight, my brow chakra, and I saw a very tall nurse dressed in a 1940's outfit and she approached me with smiling eyes. She held out her hands as I looked at them. 'You can take your baby home now' she said and as I looked there was Harry, laughing, gurgling and smiling at his wee gran. He then curled his finger around one of mine. As you can imagine, this is one of my most cherished visits from spirit, to be able to touch and physically feel my beloved Harry. I can honestly say it was truly wonderful.

My grandson, Harry then began to show up every now and then, in one meditation he crawled to me the next week his brother would, he came to me in another meditation and gave me his first word and yes the following week his brother would too and so it continues he was evolving and growing in the spirit world, so if the same person asked me now, do children grow up in the spirit world my answer would be YES!

Please remember I can only comment on my own experience never hearsay. This is very important and you need to only take on board what sits well with you and if it doesn't, then let it go, you will learn as you grow. So to develop mediumship we must learn to relax, to go into the silence, the stillness and attune with the world of spirit. Some days you will just meditate for relaxation and other days to work for the spirit world.

I would suggest you meditate at the same time each day as this will become routine, and spirit will also become aware of your connection to the higher vibrational world.

I will use a series of guided meditations which will help you relax, and I will then attune you to the spirit world, as meditation and attunement are two different things. Since mediumship is always mind to mind communication and requires some brain activity, you cannot have your brain too passive. The attunements or meditations will come after each exercise within the book as with the meditation on how to balance your chakras and clean your aura. .

To connect to the world of spirit you have to raise your vibration or energy field. As humans our energy is dense, we carry the weight of the world around with us and often become entangled in our daily lives and the traumas of the world. This fact and the physical body is why we vibrate on a heavier, denser energy.

To increase our energy we have to relax. There are many ways to do this: going for a walk; listening to music; drawing. All these activities are relaxing. But to connect to the world of spirit we have to go into a type of meditative state; an altered state of consciousness.

"We have to learn the art of meditation, Meditation takes you within"

"When meditation is mastered, the mind in unwavering like the flame of the lamp in a windless place"
Bhagavad Gita (c.500 –c.200bce)

We will do this by learning how to raise our vibration so we can pick up the energy of the spirit world. How? We will do this by learning how to attune through meditation.

Like all things in life you get back what you put in, so practise the exercises as often as you can, read, learn and more importantly, enjoy this working tool as it is to be used on your journey of mediumistic discovery, giving you the foundation stone on your quest to be the best you can be. Now that you know a little about the aura and the chakras and how they work, let's move on to the next stage.

The Clairs

There are many exercises that can be done to improve your connection to the world of spirit, many theories, but with all things practical and spiritual there are steps that need to be followed.

Through the teachings in this book you will be guided step by step.

You will learn the basics and how to connect to the world of spirit, what it actually means to be 'grounded' and how to progress in developing 'the Clairs'. The Clairs are as follows:

- Clairsentience Feeling
- Clairvoyance Seeing
- Clairaudience Hearing
- Claircognizance Knowing
- Clairgustance Tasting
- Clairofactrience Smelling

We will work on a series of exercises later in the book to strengthen your 'clairs'.

Defining you psychic/mediumistic abilities.

If you have ever used your sixth sense you have used your psychic abilities, as we are all born with six senses: five physical senses (hearing, seeing, smelling, tasting, touching); and the sixth sense, inner knowing.

It can be difficult to define because we cannot see or touch it, but inside us there is a part of us that knows. Whether we call it 'gut instinct', we just have that inner knowing that something is afoot or amiss.

Psychic abilities can cover a wide range of activities:

- Psychometry. Sensing past information from an object which it has gathered over a period of time.
- Sensing or feeling the energy in a room as you walk into it, or from a person.
- Reading Tarot cards.
- Using a pendulum or a dowser as a psychic tool.

We are all born with a sixth sense. Some people are born more attuned than others and it stays with them longer than the majority of people. Most people normally stop using their sixth sense when they reach school age and become more logical.

Some people are naturally gifted psychics and always have it, always use it. Others need to work at it, work at closing themselves to the out side world and its distractions, phones, I pods, television, radios, there is no silence, no time to listen to your inner self, think of life forty, twenty years ago, not so many distraction and better mediumship standards! Being psychic does not automatically mean you are a medium, as not all psychics are mediums. However, you will find that all mediums are psychic.

Using you psyche means tuning into earthly vibrations, tuning into other people or objects, sensing, using your aura to encompass someone by throwing it over them so your aura and theirs is intermingled, you will then begin to sense from them their feelings and anything else you wish to pick up as we discussed earlier all information is stored here, it is the same with jewellery the energy of the wearer is stored within the item and a psychic can pick it up with their aura, this is called psychometry picking up the history of the object, and the same would apply to a building you walk into or a room with people in it, you feel the energy of a place, feeling that something is happening by using your auric field.

You can sense what is going on with a person by using your psychic abilities this means you have to use your solar plexus which is sometime called a 'psychic pump'. Your solar plexus picks up information like radar. You can take it a step further and push your solar plexus out in front of someone (with their permission) until it encompasses them, and you can read everything that has happened to that person from their auric field.

You can also pick up things that they have dreamed about or thought about, as this will also be in the aura. You are picking it up from the incarnate soul, the living.

Being or having mediumistic skills is different from being Psychic.

It means communicating with those who are discarnate, those who are no longer living, and the energy is completely different from psychic energy. Unlike psychic ability, which everyone has to a degree, not everyone has the ability to be a medium.

Whether you are aware that you are already a psychic or that you are a medium, or whether you are at the beginning of your journey, this book will help you develop your psychic senses and, if you have the ability, your mediumistic skills too.

Now let's do this little exercise to see how psychic or mediumistic you are!

Some Light Relief

Psychic IQ test

Please answer all the questions.

1. Are you aware of the atmosphere when you enter a room?
2. Do you find that you either like or dislike a person instantly?
3. Do you find yourself finishing people's sentences?
4. Do you get upset with extreme levels of noise?
5. Are you aware of silence?
6. Have you telephoned a friend to find their number engaged because they are phoning you?
7. Did you ever have an imaginary friend?
8. Do you ever dream about things before they happen?
9. Are you sometimes aware of other people's thoughts and emotions?
10. Do you see colours around people?
11. Have you ever dreamed you could fly, or travel outside your body?
12. Do you know when someone is telling a lie?
13. Are you aware of spirit?
14. Are you quite shy?
15. Are you aware of danger before it happens?
16. Do objects move before your eyes?
17. Do you have a good sense of right and wrong?
18. Does electrical equipment go wrong around you?
19. Do you hear tapping sounds, smell tobacco or perfume when there is no one around?
20. Do you know that there is more to you than your physical body?

How did you do?

Remember it is only a bit of fun. How many did you tick?

0 -5 you have good intuition

6 – 10 may confirm that you are just a little psychic.

11- 15 may confirm you are very psychic

16 – 20 defiantly psychic and probably mediumistic

Get to know yourself.

Step One

The first thing I teach to all my students before they first sit to make contact with the world of spirit, is that they need to know their own energy first:

- You need to get to know every part, every aspect of who you are.
- Have you got pain in any area of your body? If so, recognise it and be aware of it.
- How is your natural posture? Are you a slouch or a leaner? Do you lean to one side more than the other? Or are you a soldier who sits up tall straight and alert? You need to know these things before you start.
- What noise do you make when you are breathing? Are you a wheezer? Do you make a squeaking noise when you breathe? Are you a shallow breather or a panter? Get to know these things.
- How do your hands sit when you are relaxed?

It is important that you scan your full body. Be aware of every part of you, every inch. This will take some time when you first start out, but when you get into the practice you will do it in minutes.

I want you now to be aware of your emotional state. Are you happy, sad, melancholy or indifferent to the world? Your mood will have a huge impact on your body.

Now consider your head. What is going on in there?

Are you calm, relaxed, stressed, mind going hundreds of miles an hour, anxious, head a roller coaster of thoughts, things to do, places to be?

Stop!

All this may have made you a little giddy, so take a deep breath and relax. Again, breathe in slowly: in through your nose out through your mouth, in through the nose, and out through the mouth. Concentrate on your tummy rising and falling.

That's right, relax, relax now.

So now you are relaxed again do you understand the importance of what I am telling you?

If you know exactly how every part of you feels before you go into the altered state then you will know when you are grounded back, as being grounded means being back to the state of consciousness you were in before: Beta state, awake, alert and ready to go about your daily life.

So, are you now aware of who you actually are?

Yes!

Are you aware of your whole self, physically, mentally and emotionally?

Yes?

Then you are fully aware and 'grounded!'

Step Two

Protection!

It is important that once you decide to go on your journey of mediumistic discovery that you learn how to protect yourself, psychically.

There are many ways to protect yourself and I would encourage you to practise each way until you find one that is easy and that you are comfortable with.

A 'psychic bubble' is one of the easiest ways to protect yourself and you can use this technique at all times, whether using your psychic abilities or not. I put myself in my bubble before I leave home each morning and strengthen it throughout the day as needed.

All you have to do is to imagine you are surrounded by a clear bubble of energy, like the bubbles you would blow as a child from liquid soap. This bubble is big enough to cover your entire being and strong enough to bounce all unwanted energy away from you. Ensure your bubble is above your head and below your feet, and it is stretching with you as you move throughout your day.

Some people like to use 'psychic mirrors', imagining that they have mirrors surrounding their bodies which reflect back to the person all energies that are sent from them.

Remember we each have a master spirit guide and a guardian angel that we can ask to assist in our protection.

One of the biggest protections used is 'The Power of Love'. Many people on a spiritual journey will use love to protect themselves from psychic attack, which is just negative thoughts being sent your way which you may pick up because you have opened up your spiritual body, you have expanded your auric field and fully opened your chakras so you are more aware of what people think, say or send.

By protecting yourself during meditation you are stopping anything negative coming into your space from people around you or people who know you, one of the easiest ways of doing this is by imagining you are surrounded in a blue light of protection from Arch Angel Michael (the protector of humanity) and he will surround you in this light and anything sent to you will be dispersed in love. This is a simple and easy exercise to practise.

Practical exercise you can do if you have falling out with someone or wish to send healing to someone.

This is not a meditation but a visualisation exercise using the power of thought as we discussed earlier we are all made up of particles as is our thoughts, so thoughts are things, energy and can materialise, so be mindful of your thoughts, but for this exercise we are sending positive thoughts and also visualising in our heads.

Picture the person you are having problems with in your mind's eye and send them love, what colour does love mean to you? Whatever colour comes into your head imagine the person surrounded in this colour see them floating in it like a bubble has surrounded them, see them smiling happy and full of love.

If negative thoughts come into your mind or you feel anger, or angry thoughts come back to you, just focus on love and the colour and keep visualising a happy person and a happy outcome, see yourself in the bubble with them and see the two of you happy, laughing and hugging each other and feel the joy that brings you, keep sending loving thoughts to the person, you may hear people on a spiritual path say send loving vibrations, it's the same thing as everything vibrates even our thoughts.

If you find it difficult to send love or to feel love, think of someone you do love and then allow those feelings to build, and send them to the person in question.

It is important that you try different ways to protect yourself and go with the way you find is the easiest or most successful for you.

As you begin to work with spirit it is important to get into the habit of protecting yourself, it is particularly important when you are a novice as it gets you into good working practices and although the universe works on the law of attraction "like attracts like", you never truly know someone so get into the habit of strengthening your aura with positive affirmations, in the beginning of your journey of discovery, because you will find that you open up more than you should, and will not always be aware of it right away. As soon as you have realised you have opened up to spirit it is important to ground yourself. If you are going to use the symbols as a way of setting your intension to open up and close down spiritually it is important not to use everyday images. If you decide a door is easier for you, you will have to make it an unusual shape and have a lock on it, otherwise you will open and close it every time someone opens or closes a door.

As you develop, closing down and opening up is done by intention.

In the beginning you need to be a little more practical, until you can reach that stage where you say 'open', and it is done.

It is good to set the standards in the beginning. Acquiring good habits now, will stop issues arising in the future.

When you have your symbol for opening and closing the chakras you will use your symbol to close the upper chakras which you need to imagine, sense or feel the energy from the crown chakra being pushed down to the brow chakra.

Once you have done, that close the door on the crown chakra and lock it. Then push the energy down from the brow chakra to the throat. Then, once you have pushed it down, close the door on the brow chakra and lock it. Now push the energy from the throat chakra down into your heart chakra, and close the door on your throat chakra and lock it. Now the same with the heart chakra. Push the energy into your feet and then into the ground, which will help you root firmer to mother earth, and lock the door on your heart chakra … and put the key in your aura.

Now you should be back to your normal daily self, your daily life. It is important that you do not mix your daily activities with your spiritual work. You should keep them separate and connect to spirit at certain pre-planned times.

I would also advise you to cleanse your own energy field at the end of every day, or after working with the world of spirit. It is a good habit to get into and the more good habits you get at the beginning of the journey the better. It is also important to be aware of how you are feeling each day, as when you go on this journey your own inner light becomes brighter, calmer and people may find themselves attracted to your aura or inner light and begin to off-load all their problems to you. In some cases, they can drain you of energy if you have not put up your psychic protection. Also, you could unknowingly take on some of their problems.

I tell my students to have empathy for people when they need an ear, someone to listen to their worries or health issues. Listen, nod, but do not try to problem-solve or give sympathy, as when you give sympathy you are taking on part of their worries. You begin to worry for them and it causes you stress. It is up to them to sort out problems for themselves, so they can learn their lessons and evolve. So, always cleans your aura with white light, imagine sense or feel white light pouring over you, cleansing your energy field of all that is not yours.

This story always comes to mind when I talk about people's problems:

Two Buddhist Monks were walking along a road when they came across a large puddle. At the puddle was a lady contemplating how she would get across so that her feet would not get wet. The eldest monk stopped and said to the lady, 'Would you like me to carry you across the water, madam?' The lady said 'Yes', and the older monk carried her across, much to the disbelief of the youngest monk. When the lady had walked on a little, the young monk asked, 'Master, why did you carry the lady across the water?' But the monk did not answer. This annoyed the young monk for many days until the fifth day when the young monk again said to his master, 'I cannot understand why you carried the lady across the water', and the old monk said, 'I only carried her three feet to keep her feet dry. You have carried her for five days!'

So remember not to carry other people's problems with you.

You can also try cleansing your aura once a week with white sage, you can buy white sage from any new age store or on line, this can also be used to cleanse the room you use for meditation and spirit work, go into your room and light the sage and smudge all around your aura, being careful around your hair or you can do it out doors if you are away from home you then allow the sage to go to the smoking stage so it is not on fire as such and you start to wave the smoke around the front of your body, then the sides and the back remembering to go between legs and around arms, below feet and above head, this keep the aura free of unwanted debris and has been used by the ancients Indians for as long as time itself.

It is also useful to have a space where you feel safe; the space you are going to use every day to connect to spirit. Cleanse your room on a regular basis with white sage the same as above but pay particular attention to the corners, never leave sage burning unattended!

Open a window to let out all the stuck energy, if there is any, and allow natural sunlight into the space to keep it light, physically and spiritually.

You can also grid the room with crystals to improve the energy and the connection; this is entirely up to you. When I talk of gridding a room it is about protecting a room or space where you live, work or meditate, by placing crystals in each corner of the room or at each of the windows in your home or above the doors acts as protection and helps with the flow of energy and is use a lot in Feng Shui an Ancient Chinese Art of keeping the flow within a space, balancing yin and yang, you can read up on this on the internet, but the basics are about removing clutter, using colour and crystals as well as the positions of items in the directions of the compass and the elements, too big a subject to cover here as this is another book in itself.

Using Crystals For Protection

You would first of all clear the space of clutter, unwanted items and open the window. I always grid my space with Kyanite and place a piece in each corner of the room because it is a high vibration stone which helps raise consciousness and brings about a feeling of tranquillity, Kyanite is also good for stimulating your psychic abilities and intuition. You can use whatever crystal you are drawn too.

Here are a few examples:

Aura Quartz - Frees your mind from limitations you may have set it also creates space for new things to happen and brings deep inner peace.

Lemurian seed crystals - Powerful communicators for working with spirit guides, these crystals are said to contain the knowledge of the ancient Lemurians.

Larimar - is a spiritual stone that opens you up to new dimensions, it radiates, love, peace and promotes tranquillity, position on third 3rd eye, solar plexus or heart charka, gently stroked down the body it removes attached entities and clears out the meridians and draws out pain.

Moldovite - Experience Spiritual realms and enhances clairvoyance. Helps you to experience and become aware of higher vibrations that those on the physical plane.

Moonstone - Good for tuning in your reception for messages from the spirit world and increasing intuition, also good for woman who are menstruating and menopausal.

Turquoise - is a most effective healer, providing solace for the spirit and wellbeing for the body. I t is a protective stone and can be worn as an amulet and will change colour warning of danger. It enhances communication and if placed on the brow it enhances spiritual sight.

Clear Quartz - is a powerful healing and energy amplifier, it stores, releases and regulates energy and is excellent for unblocking it. Needs cleansed regularly

Snowflake Obsidian - Balances you in mind, body and soul. Heightens your ability to reach your inner self and was also one of the first crystals used for scrying

I use a Black Obsidian Sphere which is speckled with gold, it looks like the universe and I love scrying with it. This is a stone without boundaries or limitation as a result it works extremely fast with great power, it helps you visualise your soul purpose and eliminates blocks in your energy field helps bring spiritual integrity.

Bronzite - It is a good protection stone, clears away confusion and helps you to adapt to your new path.

Cleansing & Charging Crystals

Cleansing Crystals

Crystals will pick up energies and vibrations from the people who have handled them before you and it is beneficial that before using them they are cleansed. It is also important to cleanse your own working crystals on a regular basis.

There are lots of different ways to cleanse crystals and it is important that you find and work with a way that feels good for you. Some of the ways that crystals are cleansed include:

- Smudging (Passing the crystal through the smoke of burning sage)
- Sea Salt Baths (beware some crystals may not react well with water or salt, Kyanite is one of these)
- Grounding (Burying the crystal in the earth for 24 hours)
- Full Moon (Placing the crystals in the light of a full moon overnight)

Once the crystal has been cleansed it needs to be programmed for the work that you want to do with it.

The simplest way I have found to programme a crystal is simply to hold it in your left hand, take yourself into a deeply relaxed state and set your intension and purpose for each particular crystal, see your heart chakra open and imagine the energy flowing down your arm and into the crystal. Crystals can be used for protection healing to remove block and as an elixir, check the crystal book before drinking an elixir.

Crystals are supposed to pick the people they want to work with rather than the other way about, so always hold a crystal before you buy it and see how it feels to you, if you don't like it put it back.

I have covered protecting yourself whilst out in the world and cleansing yourself from other people's energies, as well as how to cleanse and protect the room you will work in. Now we need to look at what we need to do as we sit ready to connect to the power of spirit.

When you are ready to sit in the power it is important that you say a prayer of protection or set a positive intention, to protect your space and yourself while going into the alpha or an altered state. This is a must whether you are own your own or in a group setting. You should always say your own prayer of protection. Get into the habit of it and never wait for anyone else to do it for you.

I would say something like:

Divine and loving universe, father and mother of all things, I ask as I sit here to connect with the higher side of myself and the greater beings of light, that you protect my space at this time, in love and peace and for my highest good. All this we do in and through your name which is divine and eternal love, Amen.

You could say your own prayer of protection calling on higher beings, the four winds, the archangels … whatever you use or believe in. But always add ‘for my highest good’, the reason we set intensions whilst we work with spirit is that like attracts like and if we tune our mind set before we go into a meditation then we are tuning our radio waves as it were to the frequency we want to be listening to. If everything is done for your highest good then you are attracting positive energy around you. It is very important to do this, especially if you are sending absent healing or thoughts to another, as the universe always knows what is best for someone before we do so, always set the intention to work for the highest good of yourself and others.

Step Three

Sitting in the power

One of the first things we will do is to sit and connect with the power and love of spirit, for no reason, other than opening your heart and sending out love to the universe. You will be surprised how rewarding this can be.

Sitting in the power can become addictive. When I first started, I wanted to connect as much as I could, as the feeling always left me euphoric.

I will say to you now, and I will remind you periodically as we go on our journey together, that discipline is, very, very important.

If you start as you mean to go on then you will be fine.

I want to share the most profound experience I had as I sat in the power. I have studied many religions over the years looking for 'God' or that Great Spirit. And it was while studying Wicca that I had an amazing out-of-this-world experience.

I am a very good student and follow what I am told to the letter. Well, I am a Taurus with my moon in Virgo attention to detail is important to all Virgos.

I drew my circle with salt for protection and lit my four candles, each representing the four directions. I had my athame and my chalice representing male and female deities, and I placed my offering in my circle and stood with the only gifts I was born with. I opened up my circle as instructed and sat in the lotus position, sending out pure loving thoughts to the universe. Bear in mind this was my first time performing this ritual so I had no expectations, other than to be a good student and complete my homework.

What happened next changed me forever. There was a profound stillness, an indescribable sweetness and a tingling throughout my entire being. I opened my eyes thinking something was wrong around me. There was such a bright light that I had to close my eyes and a feeling of pure, overwhelming love, so incomprehensible that it was beyond feeling or description.

I was aware I was being held. As I opened my eyes I was literally in the arms of an angel, male in form, no sex organs; pure, brilliant, so tall and muscular that I was the size of a new-born in his arms (and I'm no light weight). He communicated to me with such intensity that my eyes cried tears of joy, not just at that time, but for days afterwards. He told me my life would change, that my work was to heal people through words.

I didn't understand what or why this happened, but it did. I told everyone I met for weeks, months and still do of this 'OMG' moment. People used to walk the other way or cross the street when they saw me coming, incase I told them about my experience again and that is how I became 'Angel Anne', by family friends and now clients. All of this from sitting in the power!

I cannot guarantee such a profound experience for you, but sitting in the power is a magnificent experience.

I have had so many wonderful experiences sitting in the power of spirit and as I discussed earlier my grandson, Harry coming to connect with me was beautiful, in fact I may well go on to say it was even more profound than my angelic experience. However that was before Harry was born and before his father met his mother, at that time it was the best and is still one of my top ten spiritual encounters. Every experience is unique and with it bring great joy, and I am sure you will have your own experiences along the way.

I also had the privilege of sitting in a physical circle and have heard direct voice seen ectoplasm and felt that wonderful power that it brings and had a conversation with my father, a conversation, not a message and he has been in spirit for over twenty-five years.

When you are learning something new you are excited and want to talk about your experiences but I would encourage you not to discuss that you are developing as a medium because you will find that once people are aware of what you are doing, they will soon try to drain your energy by asking you questions about their requirements.

People are selfish and do not realize that asking you to perform at the drop of a hat, is intrusive. Try to only discuss it with like-minded people.

I can only tell you what I have experienced in this world and the next, I have had to learn that being spiritual does not mean you allow others to take from you, wither it is only time or effort, we have to learn discipline as usual I had to learn the hard way. As a 'sensitive' you want to help and please people' and if you let them in with a little, 'Oh, I can do a reading for you to help you with that', because you have sympathy for them, and you open up and give them one little message, that's it! They will pester you for life.

Remember what I said: give empathy, a listening understanding ear, but it is their problem to solve and to learn from. If you give sympathy you are taking on part of their problem, it will be a drain on you.

Do not allow this to happen. Be strong and confident about your development and if someone finds out you are developing and they ask for a reading, or say to you 'What do you see for me?' you can reply with confidence:

'I am training at the moment, but once I am confident that I can give you a sound and clear message, I will give you the details of when I will be working and what I will be charging.'

Treat yourself as the apprentice and when you are ready, spirit will tell you. They will let you know you have passed and you will be certified by spirit. Then you can pass on the energy from spirit to spirit for an energy exchange. Do you want to try it? But remember, you definitely don't want to become what I call a "Leaky Medium" giving messages at every opportunity, whether in the hairdressers or corner shop or on a bus, have pride in what you are doing as there is always a time and a place and spirit deserve respect, don't you think?

EXERCISE:

Sit upright in your chair. Scan your body so you are aware of your own thoughts, feelings and physical body.

Now call in your protection with a prayer for your highest good

Listen to track 2 on the C.D.

If you are just beginning your journey, I would encourage you to listen to track two a few times before you move on, as getting into and sitting in the power will help you develop your connection to the world of spirit.

If you are already on your journey and are comfortable with opening, closing and connecting to the power, then continue.

I would like you to use this space to write down what you got from spirit.

Caution

. So before you rush to move forward, to get to the next exercise, I have a little warning for you all: 'Remember the tortoise and the hare.'

The idea of learning is not to race ahead, but be present, enjoy it, experience it, practise it, live it. You will get to your destination when you are supposed to, as it is already written, so you cannot force destiny.

Be present in each aspect and on every day of your journey. Enjoy each day in the presence of your own spirit, and respect and observe the journey of the other spirits around you. We all have our own journeys to take and some will travel a different path for a while, but ultimately all roads lead to the same destination, home to the spirit world, it is the journey you make that will be reflected once you get there.

Notes:

Step Four

Sensing your Guides.

What and who are guides?

Spirit guides are highly evolved beings that are a source of energy and expertise.

Guides are always learning and maturing with us on earth. It is part of their inter-dimensional training, and they will attach themselves to us to learn a particular experience so they can develop and progress as guides as well as helping us to develop a particular area, for example, Philosophy.

It is a two-way proposition: guides help us to learn and to grow; and we help them to improve their skills as guides. It is team work, each one being a cog within the wheel.

There are a variety of spirit guides, teachers, philosophers, healers and Angels.

The primary function of a spirit guide or mentor is to help protect, assist and inspire you in your spiritual evolution.

Spirit workers/guides come in many forms, including departed family and friends who continue to watch over us.

Guides/workers usually appear in dress that is easily recognisable, e.g. robes of a monk, garments of American Indians, nuns etc. One reason that so many people have Indians, nuns and monks as guides is that whilst they were on earth they did a lot of work with spirit, they overcame the need for materialism and focused within, so when they passed back into the spirit world their soul would have evolved already and the process and learning on the spiritual laws would help them to evolve to a level where guide status would be given.

The most important thing is that our guides are always aware of our needs, even when we are not. Like teachers, a guide can show us the way and inspire us to make the right decision. However, it is always up to us to decide whether or not to follow our guide's directions, as we have free will, as I discussed earlier. "Akashic Records" record that a plan was made with your guide regarding your journey here on earth

Here is a brief summary of who and what guides and Angels are.

A Master Guide/Teacher is involved in our everyday spiritual growth and wisdom, and has been with us throughout our many incarnations. They continue to teach us lessons that are necessary for our spiritual growth. Think of this guide as part of your soul family. You and your master guide agreed to work together prior to your incarnation. Often you will feel a great affinity, as if you were a part of them. The job of the master guide is to inspire, guide and teach, as well as guide and direct us to our destiny, or soul journey, here on earth.

My own master guide has given himself the name of Alchemeds. He has a strong but subtle energy and is always very close during my teaching sessions he has tremendous love and an unwavering devotion. Last but not least is his infinite patience. He has come to my assistance many times during my emotional journey here on earth, and has not once complained about the triviality of any of my worries..

On one specific occasion my second marriage had come to an end and I had given up a good management role to buy a franchise which went bust taking all of our savings. As you can imagine, I was fraught with worry and despair as I had two children to support on my own. I used to write poetry to express my emotional state, and when I read the last one back, it was extremely dark in tone.

I cried. I had no savings, no husband and no home, but as I sat alone in my room I was aware spirit was about to visit me as the energy had begun to change. It was so quiet, so much so you can hear your own heartbeat. At that moment I saw the energy of the being, he did not fully materialise but I could see him, fear not my daughter" he said "material possessions come and go, love is the one true gift that never leaves you. "Your path is changing now as you will become more aware of spiritual law and your life purpose will come to the fore" and with those words he was gone.

It was not the words so much but the feeling he left me with as I did not understand what he meant at all, but the feeling of love and serenity was great and I knew I would be fine. At that very moment I understood both me and my children would get through this difficult period. After all, we still had our health and my mother had two spare bedrooms. Yes I could find a job as I have never been afraid of hard work. So I took up this challenge and also began my journey of healing self. Alchemeds has come to me on several occasions to show me the way and help me, never with a specific route or map but he has left me armed with a strong sense of love. He has also assisted me in other ways and I have found that I always seem to meet the right people. Synchronicity has certainly been a big part of my life since 1998.

A Gate Keeper/Protector's role is to protect our space from all energies. It is their job to first and foremost protect the medium and to bring the attention to the sitters if the medium need to be brought back from their deep altered state, they seem evaluate those from the spirit world and their intension for working with you. As on earth, there are many types of personalities and characters in the spirit world, or entities that might try to take possession of your mind. Although you are always in control, these entities can play on the weak-minded. This guide is particularly important in mediumship because of the multiple spirit energies that are bombarded at a medium's electromagnetic field, or aura. This guide mainly protects you in out-of-body experiences, the different levels of trance states and in physical mediumship circles.

My gate keeper presents himself when I sit for the development of trance. His energy is strong, demanding and he accepts no nonsense, if I didn't know he was a gentle giant, he would put the fear of God into you as his energy and force seems bigger than any of my other workers. His primary job is to protect me whilst in deeper states and he brings me back if the energy is not right or conducive to the experiment, as obviously all spirit work is experimental, and not an exact science.

Inspirational Guides assist us in learning soul lessons, such as compassion, purity, patience, understanding, unconditional love, spiritual art, writings and poetry. These guides may only be with you for a short time until a certain skill is learned. Some of these skills can be developed with a connection to your own soul too.

Helper Guides are those who are drawn to us through the universal law of affinity, or attraction; like attracts like as here on the earth plane. We attract what we need or want to learn, according to our interests at that time.

You will find that as you evolve on your spiritual journey some of your guides/workers will also evolve and change in accordance to your next step on your path and the lessons that you are learning/ developing, it is only the master guide which stays with you throughout your journey.

My great grandmother and my nephew are helper guides and they have taken an interest in work with spirit. When I am working during a spiritual service giving proof of life, my nephew runs to the person who needs to receive the message and if he remains with them I know a child is coming through as he holds their hand during the communication.

My grandmother comes across as a straight-talking, no-nonsense kind of woman who didn't like men very much! So, you can rest assured when she makes an appearance, I know the recipient of the message is having man trouble; my great grandmother was a psychic possibly a medium so I know she is interested in my work and comes to assist me. She ensures I get it right, so to speak and she will definitely let me know if I don't!

Angels are highly evolved beings who have not been on earth and are, on some occasions, brought in to uplift a soul on a difficult path. They are around us whenever we need them, but unlike the guides, we need to ask for their help before they can intervene. Everyone has a guardian angel and this angel is with you throughout your life. Whenever you need assistance you can ask your angel to help and guide you.

As you have already read, I had an angelic encounter of a magnificent sort! A truly, 'Oh My God' moment. However, there have been others from the angels as I studied for many years and still work with them, I have heard celestial music being played which is a powerful healing balm which moves your very soul. I have awoken from sleep after dreaming of meeting and talking to my angel with the most beautiful aroma in the room, a smell so sweet and pure, so indescribable but wonderful that it can only be heavenly. I encourage you all to speak to your own guardian angels as they cannot help you if you don't ask. You will not be disappointed.

EXERCISE :

As I said earlier the intention of this exercise is to allow you to sit in the power and try to connect to your master guide to help you to try and identify the energy of your master guide. Being aware of your own energy first and then feeling the subtle differences as the guide begins to make them known to you, remember your aura will be expanded and they will slowly enter your auric field and you are in control of how close you want them to come.

As you begin to sit in the power you will be aware of things around your energy field. In this exercise we are going to invite the energy of your workers/guides, while connecting to spirit. At first, you may not be aware of much difference, but with practice you will begin to feel the difference, and with more practice you will sense whether your worker is male or female, or you may just know. The more you talk to your worker in your mind, each time you sit, the stronger the connection will get. You will be surprised at how quickly you develop this, as your workers want to make that connection; they want you to be aware they are right by your side.

Sometimes, we will sit with a particular intention; for example, trying to find direction or help with a question we have, you should always sit with a purpose, a reason for sitting, even if that purpose is only to develop your connection to the world of spirit, for the joy of it.

It should never be a chore. Being a medium is a vocation: it is within you, through you. If you cut me through the middle, metaphorically speaking, it will say 'MEDIUM' like a stick of rock if you are a medium through and through, you should aspire to be the best you can be.

Sit in the power and ask to be guided, to be taught by spirit, and remember to ask it for the highest good of all as discussed earlier, for you and for those in the future that you will communicate information to you from the spirit world.

'What is the power?' I hear you say!

The power is step three, sitting in the alpha state, connected to the spirit world. It will take practice to stay in that state for long periods. the more you practise, the easier it becomes.

It is important when you are sitting in the power of spirit that you do not start to dictate to spirit, by saying, 'I want to develop my clairvoyance (seeing)' or 'I want to develop my clairaudience (hearing)'. This will get you nowhere.

We are all unique. We all have different gifts and strengths.

The biggest gift you can give to the spirit world is your trust; trust them and sit for the love of it, and watch, wait and see how you will blossom.

One thing I will say to you all now, that you cannot become a medium overnight, you cannot develop instantly, and it takes time and patience.

Each step is part of the journey in your development as a medium and you should enjoy each stage of that development, as these experiences are unique to you at that time.

The intention for this exercise is to connect to your own spirit initially and then to invite your spirit team forward, so you can get to know the difference in energy.

- What is the intention of sitting now?
- Remember set the intension like tuning in the radio
- Do you have one?
- Does there need to be one?

Sometimes, we sit with a particular intention; for example, trying to find direction or help with a question we have, or trying to contact a particular person in the spirit world.

You should be sitting each day with a purpose, and that purpose is to develop your connection to the world of spirit, for the joy of it.

If you need assistance you can ask your angel to help and guide you.

Track 3 MEDITATION TO MEET YOUR GUIDE

Sit in an upright position and scan your body, physically, mentally and emotionally.

Now you are back into your normal reality, grounded, I would like you to use this space to write down what you got from sitting in the energy with your guide and the spirit world.

Notes:

These last two exercises are the basics for building your mediumship. Once you have made the connection to your guides/workers, you should speak to them gently in your mind, asking them to teach you, guide you and show you how to move forward with your mediumship.

When you are aware that you are receiving thought communications, hear a different voice in your head, or you sense or feel different within yourself, you will know that your workers are communicating with you.

Not all of you will have the mediumistic ability of Clairaudience (hearing) spirit inside your head (subjectively), or outside your head in your real ear (objectively), but if you have the ability this will develop.

Most of you will have Clairsentience, (feeling) and some will have Clairvoyance (seeing).

The key to building a connection with your guide is patience and practice. Sit in the power and invite them in, get to know their energy and that calling card that lets you know they are with you. I would encourage you to listen to track 2 on a daily basis until you have a good connection.

Step Five

We are now going to go through a serious of exercises to enhance and strengthen your "Clairs", the six senses you use here every day are the same as you use when you are connecting to spirit. For me we have to be more aware in our daily lives, be more aware as we walk about on our daily routine; be aware of what is in our neighbourhood. Look carefully next time you head out for a walk, notice your neighbours' gardens, doors, curtains, cars; notice the colours of your surroundings, are they brightly coloured or dull, possibly in need of repair, listen to the noises of your area, do you hear birds singing, a dog barking, traffic going past, children laughing, do you smell anything? As you begin to be more aware physically, you are heightening your senses.

Being more alert and paying attention helps you be more aware and alert when you go into the altered state, these simple things along with the exercises in the book will assist you to focus on your senses and make you more aware of your physical strengths, whether it is sight, hearing, taste, smells or feeling. This will also help you know your psychic and mediumistic gifts too. Remember you use this sense daily and don't always think about it.

For example, have you ever walked into a room and felt it charged and you have known there had been a debate going on before you entered? If so, then you are are already sensing, so let's work with Clairsentience (feeling).

Clairsentience is an ability that can be used on a psychic level as well as mediumistically, as you experience the emotions and sensations that belong to other people, whether they are incarnate (living) or discarnate (spirit world). Healers are normally clairsentient. They pick up feelings of emotions and pain from their client's aura which directs them to where the healing is required.

Clairsentience, for me, is the foundation of all mediumship, as all mediums have some ability of sensing.

As we use our senses in the real world, so we use them in our connection to the spirit world, as well as our sixth sense, our intuition.

In my opinion, clairsentience is the most important facet of mediumship. A clairvoyant may be able to see a person and describe them, and this description may well fit, but it will also fit a number of people. If they have no sensing then they cannot get into the bones of the person, so to speak; they have no sense of character, personality, height or build. Sensing a person gives more information and, in general, a better description of who the person is, not just what they look like.

As a sensitive you will sense the energy when you walk into a room, sense if people have been quarrelling, are happy, or sad.

This is something you do without thinking; this is clairsentience. This is the most important facet of your mediumship and your psychic ability too.

So enjoy it and do not moan that you cannot see or hear. You can feel and, in time, other facets may well open up to you, and I am sure that they will.

You have to trust the spirit world as your journey is in their hands.

You may feel frustrated with your development but your faculties will change and develop over time.

You may have known you had the gift of mediumship at an early age, as I did myself. Many of you may have actually, physically seen, spirit materialise right in front of your very eyes — in most cases, at the bottom of your bed. This is called "Materialisation.

On the whole, some of you might have seen the spirit world materialise, including myself, I used to see spirit; spirit used to materialise right in front of me! They still do on occasion, but it is rarer now.

This can be a common occurrence at the beginning for some of you, particularly when you were a child, or in adulthood as the spirit world was trying to get your attention, trying to make you aware that you have a gift.

When you actually decide to begin to use your gifts then the spirit world usually stops materialising. Why? It takes a lot of energy for spirit to materialise and much less to communicate telepathically, in your mind.

Your gift has not left you, it has just changed a little. You may well see materialisation from time to time on your journey of mediumistic discovery. Some of you may always see it throughout your journey. As I said earlier, we are all unique.

In the exercises two and three we have attuned to the spirit world by expanding your auric field; that is, using your auric field as a sensor, as your psychic tool, or your Clairsentience.

Feeling all that comes within your auric field, in the same way as when you are in the meditative state; your aura expands and you pick up the energy of all around you.

We are going to work on a few exercises to help you develop your clairsentience.

EXERCISE:

You will need the following items:

Several squares of coloured cloth (preferably of the same material), in primary colours: red, yellow, blue, green , You will also need someone to help you as they will need to tell you how many you guessed right.

We will use the colours for the first exercise in developing your clairsentience.

Cut out two or three squares of each colour and place them in front of you, feel the colour in your hands, how does it make you feel close your eyes, how do you feel now, what does it remind you of? Place the colour on your solar plexus do you like it? Close your eyes and feel it. How does it make you feel now?

What does this colour remind you of?

Do you like it? Does it remind you of anything or anyone? Does it have a smell or a taste?

Repeat this with all the colours until you have sensed and felt each one in turn.

Once you are happy that you have sensed all the colours, then place them into a bag or hand them to your friend.

Begin this exercise,

Sitting comfortably with a friend to assist you explain the procedure to them and when you are ready close your eyes, I want you to relax mentally, take a few deep breathes. Your friend will give you a piece of coloured cloth from the bag or placed into your hand which ever you both decide on.

Touch it, feel it, what and how does this colour make you feel, tell your friend what colour you think you have, keep your eyes closed and try the next until you have tried all four, remember to keep your logic out and just go with the feelings.? Remember we are working on developing your senses so it is all about feeling!

Your friend can then give you feedback on how well you did.

If you are doing it on your own, open your eyes after each colour and assess how you have done. Remember this is an exercise to develop your clairsentience so do not be too hard on yourself, as you are working to build your sensing, and it will become stronger and clearer each time you try it.

EXERCISE:

You will need: six envelopes, and a pen, a seashell, a pebble, a flower, a feather, a piece of wood or bark from a tree.

Put each item into a separate envelope, seal it and mark what is inside each one.

To begin this exercise I want you to relax mentally, take a few deep breathes and centre yourself.

As in exercise 4 feel all the items individually and sense how they make you feel, do you like the feeling, do they make you feel happy or sad, indifferent do they awaken memories within you, once you have done this place all the items into a bag as before and get your friend to pick one out and hand it to you.

It is important that you do not try to feel physically with your fingers what is inside the envelope. The point of the exercise is to sense the energy coming from each item and how it makes you feel.

Try not to allow your physical mind to come into the exercise, as you want to use your sixth sense. Your eyes should be closed or blindfolded if you have a friend with you. Now choose an envelope from the bag.

- Feel how the energy in your hand reacts to this item. Does it feel warm or cold?
- What does the vibration feel like? Is it high or low?
- Does the energy feel light or heavy?
- Do you taste or smell anything with this item?
- Does it bring back memories of any kind?

If you are doing the exercise on your own look at what is inside the envelope after you have finished sensing.

Write down how each item made you feel. Keep these notes together for reference, as these items may make you feel different on another day.

You will, or should still be able to, feel what it is by the energy vibrating from each item. These exercises are to help you build your sensing ability, and the more you practise, the better you will become.

EXERCISE :

This exercise is a little more complex as I want you to start to sense people. Get your friends to place pictures inside envelopes.

You will have to ask them to give you a mixture of male and female young and old, it is better if actual photographs are used as they contain energy If you have no one to give you pictures, then you will have to cut some out from magazines: three pictures of men; three pictures of woman; and two pictures of children, one male and one female.

Place them all in individual envelopes and write the name or description of the person on the envelope. Place the envelopes into a bag and give them a good shake.

To begin this exercise I want you to relax mentally, take a few deep breathes and centre yourself.

Try not to allow your physical mind to come into the exercise. You want to be using your sixth sense.

- As before, close your eyes and pick an envelope from the bag.
- What does the vibration feel like? Is it high or low?
- Does the energy feel light or heavy?
- Do you taste or smell anything with this item?
- Does it bring back memories of any kind?
- Do you feel masculine or feminine?
- Do you feel tall or small?
- Do you feel young or old, fat or thin, healthy and fit, or tired, lethargic?
- Sense and feel the envelope until you cannot get any more information from it.

Once you have finished you can open your eyes and see who was in your envelope, and assess how you done, it takes time and patience. Look at what you got right, not at what you got wrong, and build on it each day.

You are now aware of how your sensing works with colour, energy items and people, as practised in the last three exercises. Are you ready to go into the power and sense and feel those from the world of spirit?

In the next guided meditation I want you to imagine that once your aura has expanded, there are thousands of little sensors on the end of it, like tiny wisps of hair or tentacles, so sensitive that they can pick up sound, movement, temperatures and feelings.

If you are aware that you are doing this and can keep focused on relaxation, you will be amazed at how much you pick up. Once you have achieved this, this exercise will become invaluable as you will start to pick up more each time you do it.

Like the exercises we have just practised, you will sense energies coming into your own energy.

You should begin to sense male, female or child energies, as well as physical feelings of how they passed. Just remember that if you do pick up physical feelings of how people passed, thank them for the feeling but then tell them to take it away, as these are not yours but theirs.

It is also important to remember what I said earlier, that you need to know how you are feeling before you go into the power.

We all feel different each and every day. Some days we are happier and healthier than others, and we need to remember how we feel before we go into this exercise, as it is important that we are using our logical mind so we know when we are feeling spirit, and not letting our imagination work overtime.

Some of you may well be aware of a feeling of cold about your body when you go into the power in this exercise. This is perfectly normal. They are called 'psychic breezes'; a cool air around the knees or shoulders, or it could be that you left a window open so please remember to check all of these things too, as it is important to keep focused on what is coming from the spirit world and what is not.

Some of you may be aware of psychic 'cobwebs' on your face in this exercise (hair-like strands on the face). This is common. If you do not like it, ask the spirit world to take it away. It is also possible that you will feel the spirit influence drawing very close and can feel the strength, height and breadth of the spirit communicator. You may also be aware of smells and tastes.

It should be an enjoyable experience and if you feel uncomfortable at any time, stop. You are always in control. Bring yourself back, ground yourself and go about your business as normal.

I think I have covered all the possibilities, so are you now ready to listen to the attunement and go into the power to develop and strengthen your Clairsentience?

Track 4 Meditation to develop clairsentience

Wiggle your toes and fingers and breathe until you know you are back in your own reality. You are grounded.

I would like you to use this space to write down what you got from spirit.

Notes:

Step Six

Exercise to strengthen and develop your Clairvoyance (seeing).

One form of Clairvoyance, a gift which some of you may well already have to some degree, is being able to see inner visions or the spirit world physically. Most people who are clairvoyant will often have another psychic gift as it does not usually come on its own.

One of the best ways to understand how clairvoyance works is to practise it yourself.

Clairvoyance isn't always as easy as it sounds, as the spirit world often use symbols as a way of communicating, and it can take a while to learn how to decipher these symbols.

I tell my students that it is like learning a new language; spirit will always use what is in your mind to communicate with their loved ones. So the symbol you are being shown will have a particular meaning for you and a different meaning for me, so you have to remember many things on this journey. You will feel like a juggler at times with several balls in the air, trying to keep them going without dropping any, but with patience and determination you will get there.

There are plenty of practical exercises that you can do to improve your visualisation skills, and you can practise on a daily basis, as the more you practise the better the you will become.

If you are a visual person then clairvoyance will be second nature to you. If you struggle with visualisation then we can work on improving it.

We are going to try to improve to improve your visualization skill with a serious of exercises. The first one is to try to visualise famous landmarks throughout the world.

EXERCISE:

Let's try this together. The Eiffel Tower will be our first building. Close your eyes and try to see the Eiffel Tower in your mind's eye. Relax and look at the picture in your mind. How easy was that?

Was the picture clear and solid, or was it hazy, like looking at it through the sun?

Did you see it at all? Or did you just have a sense of it?

If you found that you did not see anything then keep trying; it might just take time.

The next famous landmark will be the Statue of Liberty.

Let's try it again, close your eyes and picture the Statue of Liberty.

How was the picture this time?

Was the picture clear and solid, or was it hazy, like looking at it through the sun?

Did you see it at all? Or did you just have a sense of it?

These simple exercises will help you to develop your inner vision and assist you with the detail of the structure.

Once you have mastered objects the next thing is to try and visualise people.

People are more difficult to remember as we have many different pictures in our mind of how people look, at different periods of time.

For instance, if I ask you to close your eyes now and visualise your mother, what would you see?

Would you see her as she is now? Or maybe as she was when you both experienced a happy moment together?

If your mother has passed, how do you picture her? Happy, ten years younger than she actually was before her passing? Or perhaps how she was before her passing?

This part of visualisation is the most difficult and it will take time to master.

Let's try some visualisation.

EXERCISE:

The first person we will try to visualise is the Queen. Close your eyes and try to visualise. What do you see? As with the other visualisation exercise question yourself on how clear each image is and work on improving it.

Now try the President of the United States of America, Close your eyes and try to visualise. What do you see?

Try and visualise a very famous person who is important to you who has died.

Close your eyes again and try to visualise that person. How was that?

It was easier, or it should have been, because he/she has passed and the picture we see portrays their existence. It is probably a repeated visual image used over a period of years in the media.

This will be an on-going exercise for you to use to develop your clairvoyance, as you are flexing your visualisation muscles each time you use it.

Some of you may already be clairvoyant. Some of you may be aware of pictures that come into your head when you talk to people, or when you close your eyes, you see subjectively; that is, clairvoyantly

But we need to develop this so it can become stronger.

Let's try another exercise before we go into the power.

EXERCISE:

I want you to visualise your front door. Can you see it? Now scan the picture in your mind and look a little more closely. What can you see? Can you see the marks, the handle, the knocker?

Now go outside and look at your door. How accurate was that picture? Give yourself marks out of five.

Now we are going to take this exercise a little further.

I want you to think of someone you are friends with but not someone you see every day maybe someone you write or e-mail but only see them two or three times a year

Once you have decided who you will be focusing on, I want you to visualize their front door. Focus on it see it all; paint, marks, every detail. Now open the door. What do you see? Are you in a hallway or have you entered a room?

What is on the walls? Are there pictures, and are the walls painted or papered?

Now look at the flooring. What does it look like? Is there anything sitting on the floor? What is to the left of you? Is there a door or a room?

I want you to scan this whole house, going into each room and seeing what is there. You are not remembering but visualising the rooms, building up your inner visions.

Practise this exercise using different houses each time. Remember, you want to see the objects not remember them, as this will help you in the development of your clairvoyance.

Track 5 Meditation to develop clairvoyance

I would like you to use this space to write down what you got from spirit. Are you aware of any difference in how you saw things in your mind before you connected to the power? Or in how you saw them once you were in the power? Was it easier to see, or was it more difficult?

Notes:

One of the most difficult things to do when you are in a meditative state is not to use your brain!

This is a task you may well struggle with for the rest of your life (maybe not), because when you are in a meditative state, relaxed and focused on your inner vision (your clairvoyance), when an image starts to comes into your head you will automatically try to see what it is. You focus on the detail of the picture, but when you do this you are using your brain and inevitably push the picture further away.

Another mistake we make when visualising pictures whilst connecting to the power is, that we try to analyse them. For example, if we see a branch and it breaks we say to ourselves 'What does that mean?' Before you know it you are thinking, 'Is this a break-up, a split', or 'Someone is carrying a burden, causing them to break down'.

It is not for you to analyse what you are being shown. You should write it down once you have finished, and wait and see what comes about. When the relevant incident happens you will be made aware of the branch and it will fit.

That's it. No more. This picture may well have been for someone around your family and will have meaning for the person it was meant for, but not for you. Again, with practice, you will learn to go with the flow, allowing images to float in. And at the end of your meditation you will write down what you saw and, in time, you will understand the pictures. It is all part of your development.

The last exercise should be practised regularly, as the more you practise the exercise the more it will help your inner vision, your clairvoyance.

I want you to repeat this exercise at least another three times or so, so you are comfortable with it.

EXERCISE :

When you are comfortable with this exercise I will then get you to do the same exercise again but this time, before you go into the meditation, you should ask spirit a question first.

For example: I bought loads of Christmas presents over the months and I put them in lots of different places for safe-keeping and I lost one. So

I got into the power and visualised the gift I had bought for my friend, and I asked spirit to show me where it was, I focused on the packaging, relaxing not trying to force things to happen, and I was shown were it was.

I want you to try this for yourself. Small things first and see how you get on. The secret is not to force it, just allow it to come to you, and it will.

Clairaudience

We can also help ourselves to develop clairaudience, by beginning to listen more closely to people as they talk to us, not just listening to what they have to say but how they say it. If it is appropriate, close your eyes when listening to someone talking and sense their vibration, you may become aware that the person is not what they seem, they may naturally appear in control and confident but sometimes when we listen closely we can hear a little uncertainty or possibly the opposite. It is quite possible they seem quiet and just get on with their business, but when you truly begin to listen and become aware of their vibration you may find they are a confident and self-assured individual. You can practice this with friends and other students, have a poem for people to read and as you all take turns in reading everyone else will listen and give feedback on your vibration. Once you are aware of this it will help you in your development as well as your everyday life.

Again I would ask that you practise this a few times with different questions. You can still use track 5 on the download.

Notes:

Step Seven

Reading for others.

Now you have focused on clairvoyance, getting pictures in your mind's eye, I am now ready to take you to the next step.

In this next exercise, I will be discussing with you how to go into the psyche of your sitter, going into their auric field if you like. We will send a part of ourselves into them, connecting together like two wires, two becoming one, so that the information will flow from them to you.

EXERCISE :

When sitting in front of the person you are going to read, make sure you are both comfortable and relaxed. The first thing I would like you to do is to ask you to take the sitter's hand so a physical connection has taken place. Now visualise your energy going up their arm and into the person so you have a sense of what they are about.

Be aware of your own solar plexus and push it in front of you towards the sitter, and encompass them in your energy from your solar plexus. Focus on your third eye, your clairvoyance, and you will start to see pictures, symbols. Remember what that symbol means to you. What are you sensing, feeling? Give your sitter all this information, everything you are picking up about your sitter.

It is important that you give all the information to the sitter as you are getting it.

If you can visualise with your eyes open then do so, as I would also encourage you to try to keep your eyes open as much as possible. You can focus on a point on the wall and look at the sitter as you get information, then focus on the wall and wait until the pictures start coming into your mind.

You can continue giving all the information you are getting until you feel you have no more to give, and then you would finish your psychic reading.

Mediumship Reading

If you are giving a mediumistic reading then you will approach the exercise a little differently. You can still take the sitter's hand, but this time you will go into the power.

It is important at the beginning of each sitting that you are aware of the type of reading the sitter wants, but also that you are aware of the difference in the energy that you are using when connecting to a person, as each faculty is different. It is important to know if you are working on a psychic level or a mediumistic one. So you need to be aware of where the energy is coming from.

How would you do this?

You will use your clairsentience, your auric field, to sense if the energy is coming from the front, side or back. If the energy is coming into your solar plexus or the front of you, then you are working on a psychic level and you can give a very good reading on this level.

If you are working on the mediumistic level then, in general, the energy will come from the back, or to the side of you. You will be aware that words are coming into your mind and that your sensing abilities are picking up an energy in your own auric field. You will be able to give your sitter a very good reading on this level.

EXERCISE :

When giving a spiritual/mediumistic reading from a deceased loved one it is important that you give evidence of survival; evidence of who the person is. It is not evidence to say I have a mother figure with me and she is saying ....etc.

You need to be more specific and give more information so there is no doubt of who the woman is in the sitter's mind.

If you feel you have a woman, say so. Then go back into the power and sense her height, build, condition she passed, giving the evidence as you are receiving it.

Go back into the power again and sense her personality, her dress sense, hair colour, or style, colour of eyes. Was she a quiet woman or outspoken? If she gives her name, that's great. The name must be hers or it is not evidence.

Once you have given this information to your sitter and they have no doubt who this woman is, then go to the message. Why she has come forward today?

If, during the spiritual/mediumistic reading, you sense someone else coming into your energy, then you have to start the same procedure as before, and give a description of who the person is: male/female, height/ build, personality etc.

Remember, the name is only evidence if it relates to the person you have just described. If you get a name and you know it is not relevant to the person you are communicating with, you can give it if you have information on why they are giving it to you.

For example: if the spirit world drop the name "John' into your psyche or thoughts and you ask your recipient if that was the person name (with whom you are giving evidence of) and they say no, then you have to find out why the spirit world gave you that name! Do you understand? Do not dismiss it, as it will be important, ask the recipient can you understand why I am being given the name John, when they reply yes, then you would ask your spirit communicator (the person who gave you it) why? You would ask: who is John? They would then tell you who he was and the relevance of bringing him up. Once you have established the reason and the relevant information then that would also be classed as evidence.

It will take a great deal of time, effort and understanding on how the spirit world works.

As with life we all go about our business differently, so it is safe to say that the spirit world is no different.

When you are connecting to a spirit being who was a great communicator on earth then they still will be great communicators now, as the personality does not change. If they were not good at communicating then they still won't be, and your job will be more difficult as you will need to coax information from that spirit being.

It will take time to develop all your spiritual faculties — Clairsentience (feeling); Clairvoyance (seeing); Clairaudience (hearing); Clair cognizance (knowing); Clairgustance (tasting); and Clairofactrience (smelling) — and your faculties will change from time to time. When you suddenly experience a change in your ability as a clairvoyant, do not worry. You will soon realise that spirit is working on a different area and another faculty will become stronger.

You may well lose faculties such as clairvoyance, clairsentience and clairaudience, but do not worry; spirit will be working on you clair cognizance.

I will say to you now. Never panic as spirit will never leave you.

When you can stand up to give evidence of life after life, knowing your three 'clairs' have gone, and you trust the world of spirit, your clair cognizance, thoughts are all you have. You have to trust that what is in your head is the words of spirit and when you have that trust in them, and they have that trust in you, all your spiritual faculties will return; stronger, more connected than before, as you and spirit have become one, a communication for the highest good of the whole.

You will not need to worry about that happening to you for a few years yet as it will take time to build each faculty.

So are you ready to go to that next step, are you ready to start to build your house of knowledge on your strong foundations as we go to the next step? Now we are going to do a very similar exercise to the one we have just completed, but with a little more knowledge and a little bit of experience let's see if this is any easier.

Mediumship Reading 2

With this step you will need to have a friend or relative with you, or a piece of information from a friend that you are going to focus on.

The first thing I want you to do is relax. This is only an experiment, so do not put pressure on yourself, if you get something fantastic, great, if not then we can try another day or a different question.

If you do not have a person to read for, it is important at this stage that you have a tape recorder handy, or someone to write down what you are giving, if you are working on a question from someone else. So before you go into the power I want you to be clear on who and what you are working with on the earth plane, who is your recipient, and be aware that you will be working with your clairsentience and your clairvoyance.

EXERCISE :

Concentrate on the seeing at this time, but try to be aware of your aura and what you are feeling too.

If you have a visual aid you use when you focus on the brow chakra then use it, i.e. TV screen.

If not focus on the space between your brows and allow thing to come in. The difference with this exercise is you are going to give off what you see to the person in front of you, or to the tape recorder. Do not analyse what you are seeing. If you see a frog and it is pink, then say, 'I see a pink frog'. Do not let your mind change that to a girl frog.

I would suggest that you have this meditation on your mp3 player so you can have the earphones in as you do not want to confuse your recipient.

Have you got your tape recorder on or someone with you?
Do you have the subject you are enquiring about clear in your mind?

Track 6 Meditation to communicate with the spirit world

When you have stopped seeing, end your session.
I am sure you received lots of information.

It's time to receive feedback; not to analyse it, but to remind yourself of what you saw and felt and then get feedback when you can from the person you were reading for.

Once your clairvoyance develops and you learn to keep you out of it, your sitter will be able to give you feedback on your progress, on the evidence of survival that you have given them.

There will be times when you get things shown to you, that maybe you need to filter a little, as sometimes it would seem harsh to give them out in a 'raw' state, so to speak.

You have to remember one very important rule once you go on your journey of mediumistic discovery: you are responsible for your communications, both psychic and mediumistic.

Personal Responsibility

When you are giving a clairvoyant reading to a family member or to a friend it should always be uplifting; the person should never leave with a feeling of impending doom.

If you pick up something negative, you soften the blow, and always finish with something positive.

- I am not asking you to lie to the sitter but to be diplomatic.
- You must never predict a death, as you are not God.
- You must never ever tell someone that they have little time left here on earth, as you are not God.
- You never give medical advice; you are not a doctor
- You must never suggest that someone eat or drink anything as there may be underlying health issues.

This will come with experience and time. Start off by remembering these two little words:

'personal responsibility'

then you can be confident you are starting on a good footing for the future.

Step Eight

What is psychic?

The hardest energy to identify is the distinction between psychic and mediumistic energy.

In the last few exercises, I have talked of going into the power and connecting to the world of spirit. By doing this it is helping you to strengthen your connection to spirit and being mediumistic. I also want to discuss the word 'psychic'. Being psychic is good and most mediums are psychic, but not all psychics are mediums!

What do I mean?

When you work at a psychic level you are working in someone's aura. You are picking up information from them as everything that has ever happened to a person is stored in the auric field, including deaths.

Now when all mediums work they do, from time to time, go into the psychic level and that is okay. But how do beginners tell if they are working on the psychic level?

I would say that when you are working with spirit you will feel the power around you and, in most cases you will feel the energy coming from the back of you, and sometimes the side of you. When you work on the psychic level you are working in front of you. So it is important that you work on actually being aware of what level you are working in, it is important that you know yourself and how you work as it helps you with your own development.

EXERCISE:

Sit in your chair and have someone sit in front of you. Be aware of your solar plexus, your stomach area. Now push energy from your stomach into the other person. Push it in until you can feel their energy mingling with yours. Now relax. Allow words and pictures to come into your mind and give them to your sitter. You are working on a psychic link.

Now we are going to start again. With the same person sitting in front of you go into the power. Feel the energy from your heart expand and push it upwards. Now you will feel energy around you, from the back or sides, and start to give it off to your sitter. Did you feel the difference?

If not try again.

The word 'psychic' is looked upon by some spiritualists (not all) as a dirty word. Indeed it is not. I personally believe that when you are working with spirit, as a psychic medium your own spirit will most pick up information of the spirit of the sitter as well as the spirit world, it is natural and in some cases the incarnate spirit,(your sitters own spirit) also needs to hear information from the psyche, because we can as we connect to the spirit world and we can connect back in time we can also connect forwards, future forecasting, and at times we are filling the need of the incarnate spirit via the discarnate spirit who is communicating with us, because it is what the sitter needs at that time. With experience and practise you will get to know the difference.

I discussed earlier the different time scales it takes for people to develop and the difference in confidence levels, as we are all individuals. In life we are individuals, so it makes sense that as mediums we are individuals too.

I am a medium and a psychic and I am also a tarot reader. Tarot cards are seen as a taboo subject by certain people but, to be frank, they are a tool; they tell a story which the tarot reader gives to the recipient. As it is with all things, it is the intention of the person giving the reading and not the tools that should be criticised, personal responsibility is first and foremost, being responsible for your reading is paramount, as you are dealing with people's lives, so integrity, compassion and honesty must be a big part of your work.

In the early days, I find people are more confident when they have something they can focus their new gift on.

That is why I encourage people to use divination cards, angel cards, pictures, jewellery for psychometry etc. These are all excellent tools for the novice and more experienced medium as it helps you gain more insight.

Divination

The definition of the word Divination,

The practice of seeking knowledge of the future or the unknown by supernatural means.

If you can communicate with spirit and know what is happening now and they can tell you what happened in the past, and then is logical to assume they can see into the future, and they can!

Future projection is not fortune telling, as we look beyond the present and begin to see possibilities for ourselves and others we are both perceiving and receiving information from the ether, spirit or possibly the Akashic records, to read the Akashic is to read the future as well as the past.

"Fortune Telling" as it is often called can get a bad name and you have to be very careful with how you communicate what information you are receiving, you have to remind your client of "free will" and that what we are seeing is a possibility for the future but they have the ability to alter that course, how we live our lives and learn our lessons in this life time can be altered.

Some people seem to have recurring issues in their lives and don't seem to learn from past mistakes and sometimes it is up to the Medium to point out patterns and make the sitter aware and when that happens the sitter can then look at how she can possibly change her attitude to similar events in the future and how she deals with them, this then allows them to grow.

Over all it is a very difficult area to work in and you also need to be aware of your legal obligations as well as your spiritual ones.

Yet it is also very rewarding and as a medium, you have a calling like all on the spiritual path, so as a psychic and medium we inevitably will be able to see the future as well as the present and the past.

To help us get a clearer picture or for those who are at the beginning of their path there are a number of divination tools to work with and to be frank the sitter sometimes likes a focus point during the reading, you are not doing anything new, man has always sought to predict important events before they happen: early man studied the Stars as we do today with Astrology, they studied the weather patterns to know when to plant crops, we have meteorology today a little more technical but none the less it is still the ancient ways of learning about our planet.

Ancient man also studied the animal kingdom, their behaviours and patterns in movement to identify with their animal instinct as they seemed to know where to find food and shelter. Again if we look at the animal kingdom in relation to the disaster of the modern world today, there were no animals killed in the tsunami, in fact witness reports talked of the silence, no birds just the stillness and if we had still been in tune with our sixth senses then lots of lives may have been saved.

Gifted individuals from the past and the present found they could read the signs and symbols easier than others; those individuals became the medicine men, the sage, oracles, gurus, shaman. These are the same basis that we use in our divination skills today some people are natural "Seers" Clairvoyants, some still use divination tools, but we cannot ignore that we are all linked to the planet, it cannot move without it affecting us in some way and the movement of the planets have an effect on us all. Divination is the practice of predicting the future using specialised tools and rituals which have been used since the beginning of time, psychic's and medium's today as in yesteryears will at some point recognise that they are connecting to the five elements, fire, earth, air, water and spirit, as above so below, so using a tool to help you with your gifts is as natural as breathing it is how it was done thousands of years ago and it is how it will be done in the future we are in that cycle of awareness and it is the world that has changed not how we the psychic or medium communicate with the spirit, incarnate and discarnate.

As a medium I have developed such a tool to help with divination, I developed a set of cards in conjunction with an artist Michelle McLaughlin∑W, the pictures on the cards have been painted in such a way that it helps with the development of clairvoyance and can be used when connecting on a psychic or mediumistic level, they are also divination cards .

Once I had received the pictures that were to be used for the deck I sat with each in turn and asked spirit for the meaning, which was channelled to me, the spirit art cards where born!

These cards are an excellent tool to help you develop and can be purchased on my website.

There are many divination tools you can use.

Psychometry.

Psychometry has been used for thousands of years to help with the prediction or channelling process, the word psychometry means" the history of the object" watch, ring, coin, purse anything that holds energy of the owner or user of the object. Psychometry is a great tool to use at the beginning of development as it helps you gain information about its owner, anything can be psycromotised, but metal object seem to be more conducive to this way of divination.

The object must belong to the person you are reading or belong to the person for whom the reading is for and you would literally feel the energy enter your own and begin to give the recipient the information you are receiving, many of the old psychics and mediums were trained by learning the art of psychometry, as once you have learned the technique you can psychomitrise anything, auras, spirit etc.

Tarot Cards.

I love the Tarot and never leave home without a set in my handbag, I use this tool which is an art form itself within my readings, Tarot is accurate and scientific, it is a story board of the person you are reading.

The tarot has been a divination tool for hundreds of years and can be traced back to the early fifteenth century. The tarot tell a story of the Fool (the recipient) and his/her journey through life the twenty-two major arcana tell us about the significant events and issues of the recipients journey at the time of pick and the significant factors to come.

The minor arcana are four suits; the first is Wands which represents spring and negotiations of one kind or another, work, business and travel. The wand cards are illustrated as a sprouting branch and so many of them refer to the beginning of new enterprises. Wands represent brown haired, light skinned people and represents fire signs Leo- Sagittarius and Aries.

Cups are associated with romance, marriage warmth and friendships, possessions and long term education and represent the summer months, the idea of fullness, fruition, warmth and joy which fit well with the lazy days of summer and represent blonde light haired people and the water signs Cancer- Scorpio and Pieces.

Pentacles are associated with money, and matters relating to the question of status and possessions such as property, goods and organisation of business, building for the future, and represent the Autumn and fit with the idea of bringing in and storing the harvest, the cards give a feeling of wealth and resources. Pentacles represent very darks skin and dark hair and it also represents earth signs, Taurus – Virgo and Capricorn.

Swords indicate trouble and strife, health issues, sadness and betrayal, authority figures, travel, swift action required. Swords cold steel represents the winter months, and represents sadness, loss, pain, fear and rejection, dark hair, dark complexion people, and represents Air signs Gemini- Libra and Aquarius.

The Court card are characters within the recipients life past and present, Kings are mature men of at least 35 years of age, possibly older. Queens are adult women 35 plus years. Knights are androgynous and represent young adults both male and female ages approximately 16 to 35 years old. Knights represent change.

Pages are young children again androgynous and represents young children both male and female ages from birth to 16 years, these cards bring about news. The tarot is a combination of Astrology, numerology and symbolism and can be a very accurate tool, learning to read the tarot can be a life's time work and is an art in itself.

Palmistry.

Palmistry and indeed face and other body parts have been used since the beginning of time as a divinatory source, palmistry is still widely used today and can be associated more with gypsies and travellers it is an art form but can be passed down through generations within the travelling communities. Palmists believe that the lines, creases and markings on the palm of the hand and fingers reveal aspects of our personalities, and tell a story of our past present and future. Rather than just random lines, the subtle form of palm reading is more complex than the common held fallacy.

Astrology.

One of the oldest and most widely consulted forms of divination, astrology is the study of the positions of the stars and the planets at the time of our birth shape our personalities and how the whereabouts of each of the planets in our birth charts can predict our future. For centuries, astrologers have divided the heavens into a wheel to map the movement of the planets. The wheel is called the zodiac and consists of the twelve houses. As the planets and satellites in our solar system complete their orbit, they pass through the houses of the zodiac and astrologers can tell us the influence these have over us. These predictions are known as Horoscopes and can range in detail for weekly newspaper reading, which are based on a large scale of people, to personal individual charts been written. It takes years to become an astrologer and a degree needed before you can officially call yourself one.

Crystals.

The stones and crystal which secrete from mother earth have been used for divination for thousands of years, they are natural energy transmitters, and can be used to absorb negative energy from a source and also for transmitting energy, all crystals have meanings which can be read by sensitive individual, crystal readings are not as common as the use of crystals to help heal and bring in balance to the chakras, but there are those who have taken the time to know the properties of each of the many thousands of crystals and the meaning and use this to programme and tune into these wonderful gifts from our earth as a form of divination.

As with all professions you will each be drawn to use specific tools to help you in your development, and the short synopsis on divination is but a tip of the iceberg on divination tools out there, the fact that you are psychic and or a medium is your strongest tool and the divination options are entirely an individual and personal choice.

Final words

"Lives of great men all remind us, we can make our lives sublime, and, departing. Leaving behind us, footprints on the sands of time"
Henry Wadsworth Longfellow (1807-1882)

It is important to remember when you are developing mediumship to keep an open mind, to allow things to come into your thoughts and to be aware of the changes within your energy field.

It is also important to remain practical and not to let your imagination run away with you. Always look for logical reasons for things that happen around you before thinking this must be spirit.

As I mentioned earlier, it is also important to remember to separate the two faculties of Daily Living and Connection to the spirit world.

When you combine both on a daily basis you will become tired, over-wrought, anxious. You will be completely drained of energy as people knowingly or unknowingly extract information or energy from you, and some of you may become what I like to call 'leaky mediums', mediums who drop information to people at every opportunity. See yourself as a battery and if you leave your connection to the spirit world on 24 hours a day you will soon be drained of all your resources.

I cannot reiterate this enough. You need to be two people: at work by day; and a family member by night, and a medium when the time is right. Discipline is of the utmost importance.

It is also important to remember that it will take time to develop and you need to remember that some days you will have great connections to the spirit world, the information you will receive will be wonderful, evidential, and accurate, and you will be amazed at how far you have come.

However, there will be other days when things do not go so well. You will find it difficult to settle in meditation, your clairvoyance may be poor and, on occasion, you just do not feel connected, and this is fine. You are human. We all have bad days. It is important that you do not let this get you down and take it as a learning experience instead.

I need to remind you that you are Spirit within the physical body and, at times, your body becomes overworked, which will affect your mental and spiritual bodies too.

So I encourage you to look after yourselves on your journey of mediumistic discovery, to always plan downtime, 'Me Time'. Pamper yourself with relaxing treatments; go for walks in nature when you feel stressed.

As mediumship can take its toll on your body, if you do not look after it well, as you become sensitive to the spirit world your physical body becomes more sensitive too, you may develop allergies to chemically filled food and may well need to go down the road of fresh organic products as I have had to do and so many others like us.

Your physical body will become more sensitive the more you work with the spirit world which will make your body more sensitive or addictive to certain foods, Alcohol and cigarettes if you smoke, if you are aware that this is happening then you can control it.

I gave up smoking and drinking alcohol at the beginning of my journey to help make my vessel clearer for communication, but as I stopped some habits I picked up new ones and became aware that I was becoming dependent on sugar fixes, so I now limit myself to small amounts of dark chocolate, if we are aware that our sensitivity affects us then we can take sensible steps to deal with them.

You also need to remember we are all connected to this vast universe and as it moves and flows so we do to. The moon will have a big effect on your mediumship and you should keep a diary of when the moon is waxing, waning or full and how it affects you, as we are eighty per cent water the moons pull can be strong. We are all different. On a full moon I have to re-charge, as my mediumship is poor, but some of you might be at your strongest on a full moon, so get to know how your mediumship works. Get to know how your body works and reacts to the seasons too, winter is never a great time for me as I have to work really hard to lift my energy so the seasons will have an effect on you too.

You can see therefore, the importance of keeping a log of how you have worked and if you keep a diary for three years and see a pattern emerging then you know yourself, when you are at your best and when you should have a holiday.

Women will also have to record how they work during their menstrual cycle as they may find that their cycle affects their mediumship, if we go back to the days of our ancestors women would rest for three days during their cycle. The Indians had moon lodges where woman who had their period would stay for 3 days and rest, now we are expected to take a pain killer and get on with it.

Listen to your body, get back in touch with nature as this will all help you in your development, listen to what your body needs and don't go down the road of conveyance.

Some of you may think, 'it does not take much effort to connect to spirit, so why will it affect me?'

Believe me it will. You use a lot of your inner resources, so it is important to try to eat natural foods and drink plenty of water, treat yourself well, relax, and take time out as working with your mediumship or psychic facilities is very draining on the human body, but more importantly it is also very rewarding, so enjoy your journey but enjoy good health too.

"Just as iron rusts from disuse, even so does inaction spoil the intellect"
Leonardo da Vinci (1452-1519)

After word

I sat at my computer in 2010 with the intension to write a course, before I knew it I had written 2000 words. It seemed the universe had another idea, I began writing in my usual manner as the waves of knowledge poured onto the pages, crystal clear but my mind seemed foggy, altered in some way, spirit inspired! Then during the two years it has taken me to finish, I seemed to have lost my way a little, things happen, challenges from the spirit to help me grow in some way,(soul growth). The process of writing, to finish what I had started, stopped!

I had become blocked by grief, as I got lost in trying to help my family cope, to help my son and his partner with the loss of their baby boy, I got caught up in a physical reality, which it is not, it is an illusion, but I got caught up in the material world, which is very easy to do as I am only human, I'm in an earthly existence and that's what we do.

I lost direction, focus but not my faith, never my faith. I got lost in the darkness of my families grief, and ofcourse my own, I had to acknowledge my grief too (eventually)!

The strength had slipped from my spirit within, the reality that we are spirit within a physical body and not the other way around. I tried to fill my son's home, to hold their space and fill it with love and order, quietly entering their home doing chores, cooking meals making sure their space was conducive to healing. Then one morning I woke up, I knew everything that had happened was part of the plan, the universal plan. I remembered past visions two years prior before they had my first grandson, as I saw her with another baby, not their first born Jack no another one, but it was only one and she was sectioned in that vision she wasn't sectioned with Jack. Only one baby not two, twins did not materialise, both boys were never meant to be here as twins, one here one on the other side, guiding and helping his brothers, an even greater gift. Now I am back, back in the real world which is within me, my spirit.

Looking back I now see that reality sometimes stops us in our tracks, but faith, belief in what really matters, that fusion of spirit through spirit which brings in the real power and that my loved ones are not dead to me, but are here in spirit with me, from spirit to spirit through spirit and if we can remember that and don't get caught up in the illusion of materialism then we will be part of the divine which is within us.

"I'll lift you and you lift me, and we'll ascend together"
John Greenleaf Whitter (1807-1892)

Recommended books

Teachings of Silver Birch	
Spiritualism Today	Maurice Barbanell
On the edge of the etheric	Arthur Findlay
The history of spiritualism	Arthur Conan Doyle

All of the above books can be found on the website of the SNU

Chakras	Charles leadbetter
Aura	Charles leadbetter
The modern prophet	Edgar Cayce
The essence of living by	Mary Latimer
Buddha	Deepak Choppra
Mia's world	Mia Dolan
Messages from the masters	Dr Brian Wiess
The life you were born to live	Dan Millman

Synopsis

A Comprehensive insight on how to develop your psychic and mediumistic ability, a step by step guide in laymen's terms for personal development and spiritual awareness aimed at beginners, people who have never sat in meditation or know their chakras from their korma's and to the more advanced who just need extra guidance.

The book takes you by the hand and leads you through the stages of your physical/spiritual and emotional bodies, what they are and their purpose, into the realms of the spirit world, guides, angels and family and how to achieve this connection through the altered states of awareness as well as what the altered state is.

It is a practical and pragmatic approach, hands on, with Angel Anne with you every step of the way giving reference to her own personal experiences, and possible solutions to blocks along the way of your journey of discovery.

The exercises are realistic, practical and are designed to enhance and help develop/strengthen the necessary sensitivities to become more in tune with their Intuitive/spiritual self.

At the end of each tutorial there is a guided meditation to put into practice what you have just learned and the information for your free downloads within the book.

The book continues with this thread of knowledge until we get to the final stage, reading for others and the introduction of my spirit art cards which were produced specifically to help with the development of clairvoyance, and onto divination and completion of the first road of their journey of discovery.

Have fun as life is a learning school, and it is important to remember to enjoy it.

Enjoy the journey. Work on what you have learned, but most of all ... look after the vessel which carries the communication from the world of spirit.

www.angelanne.co.uk or

ISBN Number 978-0-9573650-0-1